The Harbour View Story

by

Charles H. Turnbull

revised edition

The Harbour View Story
© 2024 Estate of Charles H. Turnbull

Cover design: Rebekah Wetmore
The line drawing on the back cover, and the cottage portrait sketches, are
by the author
Editor: Andrew Wetmore

ISBN: 978-1-998149-54-4
First edition, Longview Press, 1994
Second edition, Longview Press, 1997
Revised edition, Moose House Publications, July, 2024

Moose House Publications
2475 Perotte Road
Annapolis County, NS B0S 1A0
moosehousepress.com
info@moosehousepress.com

Moose House Publications recognizes the support of the Province of Nova Scotia. We are pleased to work in partnership with the Department of Communities, Culture and Heritage to develop and promote our cultural resources for all Nova Scotians.

We live and work in Mi'kma'ki, the ancestral and unceded territory of the Mi'kmaw people. This territory is covered by the "Treaties of Peace and Friendship" which Mi'kmaw and Wolastoqiyik (Maliseet) people first signed with the British Crown in 1725. The treaties did not deal with surrender of lands and resources but in fact recognized Mi'kmaq and Wolastoqiyik (Maliseet) title and established the rules for what was to be an ongoing relationship between nations. We are all Treaty people.

Also available from Moose House Publications:

The Harbour View Story Continues

The
**Harbour View
Story**

Continues

...which carries the story of this book forward to 2024

HARBOUR

M   MUSEUM
Po   POST OFFICE
PK   PARKING
PLAY   CHILDREN'S
TEN   TENNIS COURT
SW   POOL

NOT TO SCALE

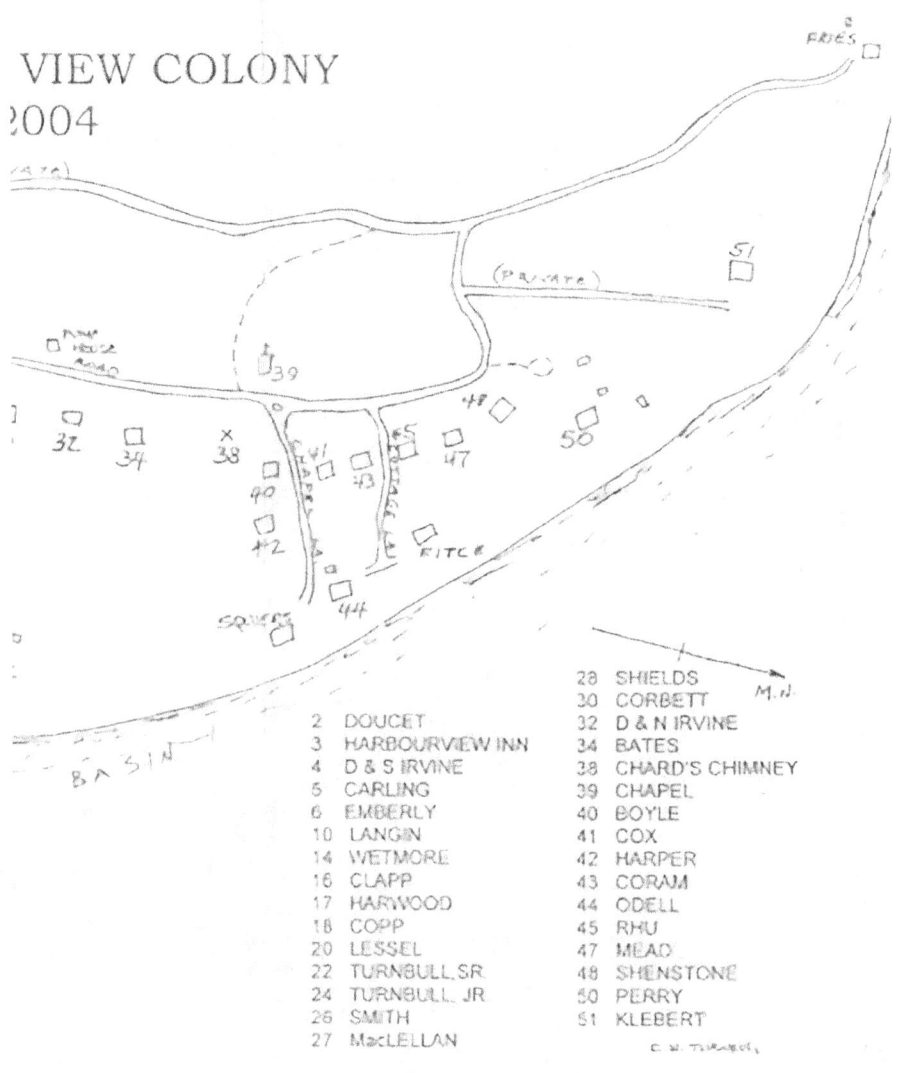

VIEW COLONY
2004

(GATE)

FRIES

(PRIVATE)

51

NEW HOUSE ROAD

39

32   34   38   48   50

40   41   43   47

42

FITCH

44

SQUIRE

BASIN

M.N.

2 DOUCET	28 SHIELDS
3 HARBOURVIEW INN	30 CORBETT
4 D & S IRVINE	32 D & N IRVINE
5 CARLING	34 BATES
6 EMBERLY	38 CHARD'S CHIMNEY
10 LANGIN	39 CHAPEL
14 WETMORE	40 BOYLE
16 CLAPP	41 COX
17 HARWOOD	42 HARPER
18 COPP	43 CORAM
20 LESSEL	44 ODELL
22 TURNBULL, SR.	45 RHU
24 TURNBULL, JR.	47 MEAD
26 SMITH	48 SHENSTONE
27 MacLELLAN	50 PERRY
	51 KLEBERT

C. W. TURNBULL

Note:

The names of the Inn and the main road among the cottages have appeared at different times as "Harbor View, "Harbourview" and "Harbour View".
This inconsistency in the text is historical, not an oversight.

To
those who have gone on before:
they are our heritage.
And to those who follow:
they are the brilliance of the future.
And to those who show the way:
they are our hope.

Harbor View

Smith's Cove

Nova Scotia

A UNIQUE & CHARMING
SUMMER HOME FOR FAMILIES
OF THE BETTER CLASS

The Harbour View Story

Harbor View

Smith's Cove

Nova Scotia

A SELECT SUMMER COLONY
ON THE SHORES OF
ANNAPOLIS BASIN

This book...

is not what I set out to make it. My first intention was to preserve a record for my children and grandchildren about what life was like here at Harbour View before World War II. From that start the book has grown to be an example of how causes and effects, places and people, are inseparable. Thus the book has become a history up through 1996 in which we, the living, are merely the part of the cast presently on stage.

I give my gratitude and appreciation to those friends who helped with this story. Each one contributed time, interest and support, as well as the information and lore that keep this work from being totally lop-sided. Putting all this together has been an unexpected delight for me.

These kind people include: Nora Saulnier, Barbara Schweitzer, Neil Boucher and Brenda Dunn, all provincial historians; Harry Sulis, Hester Bates, Jim and Jinnie Squiers, Mary Lou and Kelsey Raymond, Pat Rhu, Isabel Cossitt; Ralph Cossitt by means of taped interview; Mona and Philip Webb, Rellen Perry, Edith Lynch McClearn, Barbara Milbank VanDoren, Robert Milbank; Allen Shenstone by means of his copious historical notes and from my many conversations and experiences with him during his lifetime; Doug Irvine for suggesting the project and prodding me for several years, and by his written account of the history of Shady Grove; Nancy Irvine for her reconstruction of the children's program and activities in the casino and barn; Priscilla Turnbull for prodding, suggesting, helping and feeding me all the while; but most especially to David and Sylvia Irvine, who have lived and studied Harbour View and its lore for the past thirty years and who, by the good taste, judgment, and prudent management they have lavished upon its evolution, are largely responsible for the survival of the Harbour View legacy.

CHT

The earth beneath us

This portion is largely taken verbatim from a photo-copied page, the geologist-author of which I have not been able to identify.

Four hundred million years ago most of the earth's continents moved together, creating a "supercontinent" named Pangaea. Sediments that may have accumulated in deep water off the coast of North Africa were squeezed against the forerunner of present-day Nova Scotia, forming the bedrock here.

Beginning 370 million years ago, material several miles thick eroded from the Acadian Mountains, a high, rugged area of interior Nova Scotia that has long since been completely worn away. These sediments were deposited in a shallow basin where they gradually formed the red sandstones and shales that now surround much of the Bay of Fundy.

The break-up of Pangaea 230 million years ago caused fractures to open in this shallow basin from which lava flooded the region. North Mountain is a remnant of these ancient lava flows.

During the next 100 million years, the Annapolis-Cornwallis valley was formed when a wide band of sandstone situated between the North and South mountains was eroded by rivers descending from the Acadian Mountains. One such river, the Bear River, flowed high above the present valley floor, crossing North Mountain along a fault line. The gradual erosion of this fault line formed Digby Gut.

In the past one million years, the landscape of the Annapolis-Cornwallis valley has been further changed by four glacial periods. Ice caps from the most recent glaciers disappeared from the South Mountain only 10,000 years ago. The Annapolis Basin was created 4000 years ago when the sea broke through Digby Gut and flooded the Annapolis Valley lowlands. [That was about the time when the Old Kingdom of Egypt gave way to the New Kingdom, when Abraham left Ur in Chaldea, and when Stonehenge was the center of religion in England—just a few minutes ago, geologically speaking.]

The process of change continues today, as erosion and the combined effects of rising sea levels, sinking land and an increase in tidal range further enlarge the Annapolis Basin.

Europeans and Indians

Let us turn back briefly to the first European claims and settlement. In 1603 King Henry of France and Navarre deeded that handful of North America between the 40th and 46th parallels, roughly all the real estate between Philadelphia, Pennsylvania and Fredericton, New Brunswick, a land to be called La Cadie (later Acadia), to one Sieur de Monts. Conversion of the aboriginal inhabitants to Christianity headed the list of the Sieur de Mont's stated duties as grantee, but the development of commerce and the production of wealth occupied the attention of all Frenchmen concerned to a greater degree.

The following year de Mont's party sailed into the body of water that we call the Annapolis Basin and that they called Port Royal. Marc Lescarbot, a member of the expedition, described our beloved Basin in the following manner:

> This port is environed with mountains on the North side. Toward the South be small hills, which (with the said mountains) do pour out thousands of brooks, which make that place pleasanter than any other place in the world. There are very fair falls of waters, fit to make mills of all sorts.
>
> At the East is a river between the said mountains and hills, in the which ships may sail fifteen leagues and more, and in all this distance is nothing on both sides of the river but fair meadows. This river was named l'Équille [sand eel] because that was the first fish taken therein.
>
> The said port, for the beauty thereof, was called Port Royal.
>
> Monsieur de Poutrincourt, having found this place to be to his liking, demanded it, together with the Lands thereunto adjoining, of Monsieur de Monts. (*Nova Francia: Description of Acadia*, Marc Lescarbot).

So we see the paperwork was properly done that legitimately and legally transferred this area, together with some outlying places, from King Henry (who owned it by a grant from God) to the Sieur de Monts, and then the choicest bit of all was transferred to the Sieur de Poutrincourt. Of course, the English were not consulted and were not included as party to these real estate transactions, but they subsequently took action to issue legal deeds of their own for the same lands. At no time were the original and rightful owners consulted either by the French or the English.

Be it said, however, that whereas the French treated the native Mi'kmaq Indians (known by the French then as "Souriquois") with kindness and like human beings, the English looked down upon them as inferior beings and not fit to associate with or to learn from. This is why nearly all Mi'kmaqs are Roman Catholics today and not Anglicans. (It may also have some bearing on why the British lost a large part of North America to people who had learned the value of Indian fighting techniques and who chose not to target themselves by wearing scarlet jackets into battle.)

To develop the economic base for his newly-granted land, the Sieur de Poutrincourt brought in settlers, most of whom were peasants and artisans. The most favored lands were the salt meadows, because they were not covered with forest and brush and were easily brought under cultivation.

Dikes were easier to build than was the clearing of virgin forest without the advantage of chain saws and bull dozers. The dikes kept out the salt water, and the abundant rain and snow quickly leached any remaining salt from the soil. Furthermore, the French peasant settlers were familiar with dikes and were not accustomed to clearing forests. Not only is the clearing of land tedious labor, but much time must elapse between the first stroke of an axe and the first harvest from the soil. Harvests from diked salt meadows came more quickly.

More quickly still were the abundant and instant harvests from the sea at the settlers' front doors. Clams and mussels were there for the digging and picking. Fish were easily plucked from a simple brush weir, a device that works best in waters where there is substantial tidal action. Lobsters could be grabbed from pools at low tide or caught in simple traps.

Life was simple for the Acadian settlers for nearly 170 years. Then, in 1755, the British deported those who lived in the fertile

Annapolis Valley and confiscated their lands and livestock. The British either occupied or burned down all their barns, sheds and dwellings so as to discourage any efforts of the Acadians to return to their rightfully-owned lands.

Beginning in March 1768, 200 relocated Acadian families walked from Massachusetts Bay to Memramcook, New Brunswick. Learning that their houses had been destroyed and their lands occupied by others, many stayed there. But there were others who took the oath of allegiance to the English king and walked on, and settled on lands allotted to them in Clare, the "French Shore" of St. Mary's Bay between Weymouth and Salmon River, having covered over 825 miles on foot to their new homes.

There are no records whatsoever of Acadian settlers having lived in Smith's Cove. Instead of records there are unanswered questions—mysteries that invite speculation. Isaiah Wilson, in his extensive research for his *History of Digby County*, found no evidence of this nor did I. And there are no salt marshes here; all of them are concentrated at the northeastern end of the Annapolis Basin and up the Annapolis River.

Hazel Clayton, however, mentions in her *Down Nova Scotia Way* that Acadians were living here when Joseph Smith, the first United Empire Loyalist settled in Smith's Cove. Smith arrived in 1783. Clayton also reported that Cuthbert ("Cuppy") Welch had found two Acadian cellar holes near the shore between Kelpie, the old Bishop Jaggar place, and the Bishop Richardson place, cottage #51. (It seems that Smith's Cove, and Harbour View in particular, is a haven for Anglican bishops; valued members of the community they are, too.)

Cuppy is also reported to have found a French "gun" near cottage #35 and deduced from it that a French fort must have been there, None of these stories can be substantiated, but they make for good telling, Furthermore, a little mystery, like the faintest whiff of Chanel N°5, can bring warmth to the heart.

There remains the mystery of why the railway station here was named Imbertville. The only reference to the name Imbert is that of a Captain Simon Imbert who commanded a relief ship that brought passengers and supplies to Port Royal in 1611, soon after it was founded. It is fun to speculate that he established or financially backed a settlement in Smith's Cove, but we'll have to park that theory in fantasyland.

Early French maps don't help in the matter of place names either. The first map, Champlain's, names the Bear River as St. Anthony's River. Marc Lescarbot's map shows it as Hébert's River after Louis Hébert, the apothecary in the original de Monts expedition. Later maps show it as Imbert's River and Bear Island to be Imbert's Island. All of these cartographers ignore Smith's Cove.

Let's assume then that some high-up in the Dominion Atlantic Railway coined the name Imbertville. Because he was the boss, it stuck.

For the latter years of the Bruces' ownership of cottage #18, a sign reading 'Imbertville' was nailed to the corner of the deck. The sign is now gone and the name has slipped into oblivion.

Loyalists, Sulises and Cossabooms

Before the Loyalist days, all the land between the mouth of the Bear River and the Joggin, including Bear Island and the small island to the east of it that has long since washed away, was granted to Col. Jonathan Hoar of Concord, Massachusetts. Upon Hoar's death all this land passed into the hands of John Ritchie. As neither Hoar nor Ritchie had fulfilled the terms of the grant, it reverted to the Crown and became available for Loyalist settlement.

In 1783, the ship *Atalanta* arrived, carrying United Empire Loyalists from New York and New Jersey. Joseph Smith was among them. This was the first of the Loyalist invasions.

Joseph Smith settled on lot #10, which included the southwest side of this point, because there was a dependable stream there and a cove that was protected from northeast storms. That cove is Smith's Cove.

The following year, 46-year-old Daniel Sulis, Loyalist from New Rochelle, New York, settled on Lot #8, which included the northeast side of the point where Harbour View now stands, and all the land up to the top of Hardscrabble (Sunset Hill). These lots #8 and #10 have nothing to do with the maps of Harbour View in this book, but designate large lots on the original map of Smith's Cove land grants. Indeed, the Harbour View colony was eventually carved from lot #8.

The cove on this side is Sulis Cove. This land is exposed to heavy northeast weather coming at it straight down the Basin and the Annapolis Valley beyond.

It may be confusing, but there are two coves in the Village of Smith's Cove. In spite of its exposed orientation, Sulis Cove (on the northeast) has several advantages over Smith's Cove (on the southwest). It has the finest clam bed in the whole Annapolis Basin. In the Bear Island sandbar it has a perfect location for a fish weir of the simplest construction. And from the artist and vacationer's point of view, certainly not that of the original Sulis settlers, it has the finest light and the best views of any spot in the Annapolis Basin.

Daniel Sulis built his house where Perryford, #50, now stands. His son, John, built his where David and Sylvia Irvine's present house (#34) is. John's son, Daniel Jr., built his house where the Shenstone cottage (#48) is now.

The Sulis family operated a weir in front of what is now the Squiers' house, 34 Chapel Lane, (originally the Fritz Englehart cottage). The Sulises also had a small wharf located where the slip is shown on the Daniel Turner map of 1931. The remains of it can still be seen, but barely.

The Sulises built their homes where they did because of the abundance of fresh water available there, as is still evidenced by the numerous springs.

Descendant Charles Sulis was living in the house that later became the original Harbor View House. Charles became infirm and needed home nursing. His eldest son, Henry, was enjoying such a prosperous carpentry career in Boston that he preferred not to come home to take care of his father. Charles's daughter, Clara, who had married William Cossaboom of Gulliver's Cove, came home with her husband to care for him and to manage the farm.

Thus, upon Charles's death, the property went to the Cossabooms instead of to the eldest son, and they began Harbor View House and Cottages in 1898 with the main house and four log cabins (#236, #237, #238 and #10).

By 1912 Cossaboom found it necessary to expand the main house and in 1923 he built the Annex. The enterprise was off to an auspicious beginning.

The property thus stayed in the Sulis family from 1784 until it was taken over in default by Mr. Jefferson in 1947 (153 years!)

Daniel Sulis Jr. granted the land for the cemetery on what is now Beachcomber Lane. Two summer visitors are buried there: Locke Tiffin Shenstone and her daughter, Katherine Meade. Dr. Filbee buried his father there.

The Smith-Thomas cemetery was given by Joseph Smith and is located on Lovers' Lane. It is bordered on three sides by the campground.

Lovers' Lane was the road that formerly led to Kelpie, the Jaggar family's place. For further information on Kelpie, see *Inn and Out* by Penny Gott.

Original hotel in 1910, seen from the northeast (pre-tennis court)

1933 view from #10 cabin. Part of verandah enclosed

Better Railroad and Steamship Service for 1924

From Central Wharf, Boston, the splendid Boston-Yarmouth Line S. S. "Northland," just remodelled with 230 staterooms and space for 30 automobiles, will operate with ships already in service, daily, except Saturday.

From Yarmouth wharf the NEW "FLYING BLUENOSE" EXPRESS, to Digby in 2 hours, completes the best service ever offered in Nova Scotia.

Check baggage to Imbertville Station--50 feet from Harbor View limits--where all trains stop, except "Bluenose." Passengers by "Bluenose" will be met by Harbor View autos at Digby, (or elsewhere, if desired).

Travellers who dislike a short sea trip at night (16 hours from Boston), may take B & M. R R. trains from North Station, Boston, to St. John, N. B., thence to Digby (3 hours) by S. S. "Empress" (Auto space on "Empress" limited to 16 cars).

Automobile tourists may obtain information as to routes, maps, etc., by writing A J. Campbell, Secretary Nova Scotia Publicity Bureau, Halifax, N. S.

The Dominion Atlantic Railway Office and Information Bureau, 12 Milk St., Boston, will gladly furnish further information.

All stateroom and auto reservations should be secured in advance.

Write

Wm. Cossaboom, Harbor View,

Smith's Cove, Digby Co., Nova Scotia

R. R. Station: Imbertville.

NO PASSPORTS REQUIRED.

MAIN BUILDING

New Features at Harbor View.

An Electric Light Plant—all night service for buildings, grounds, and private bungalows throughout the colony.

A Salt-Water Swimming Pool, 60 x 100 feet, on the beach, water changing with every tide.

A Fine Annex, wide verandas, large airy rooms with private bath, electric lights, and the comforts of home for families or individuals not requiring private cabins.

A Wilderness Camp, completely furnished cabin at Sixth Lake, separate cabin for guides, deep in the woods, but accessible in 3 hours from Harbor View by auto and canoe.

A Large Dancing and Amusement Pavilion, excellent floors and good orchestra.

The Harbor View House and its Bungalow Colony is distinctly different from any other resort in Canada. From

THE CHAPEL (CHURCH OF ENGLAND)

its inception 24 years ago, a carefully exercised policy of soliciting only the most desirable class of patrons has resulted in an entire colony of people with whom it is a pleasure —even an honor —to associate. With 30 private cabins already occupied, and a picturesque rustic chapel erected by the summer guests ; with nearly 2 miles of water frontage on the famously beautiful Annapolis Basin, and dense woods in the background ; with a broad view of unsurpassed charm over the Basin, Digby Gap, the Bay of Fundy, Beaman's Mountain, and the distant Granville shore ; with the sweeping Fundy tides, the wonderful kaleidoscopic changes of atmosphere, and the incomparable sunsets ; with the delightful summer climate, invigorating in the daytime and restfully cool at night: **Harbor View is absolutely unique.**

Bungalow Sites are still available with water frontage and beautiful situation, near enough for intimate inter-

THE ANNEX

course, or remote enough for privacy—
even seclusion—as desired. There is
no crowding at Harbor View. You may
build your own cabin, or the management will build one for you at surpris-
ingly low cost.

Cabins, Fully Furnished, with bath
and electric lights, may be rented for
the season but should be engaged a
year in advance.

The Central Dining Room accommodates
200 guests. The proprietor takes pride in sup-
plying the freshest vegetables, cream, fruit, fish
and farm products obtainable in a country rich
in fertile farms, and noted for the delicacy and
fine flavor of its sea foods. Sparkling artesian
water is used. Visitors note that the service is
characterized by a genuine good will and hospi-
tality, without ostentation, and by a consistent
endeavor to provide every home-like comfort
and attention desired.

Out-Door Amusements in great variety are
enjoyed at Harbor View:—bathing, fishing, ca-
noeing or sailing on the Basin, clam-bakes, hikes
over miles of delightful and picturesque country.
Our own salt-water swimming pool, tennis courts,
automobiles, boats, saddle horses, and dancing
pavilion, with good orchestra, are available,

SIXTH LAKE CAMP

while the splendid links of the Digby Golf Club
are open to guests of Harbor View at moderate
fees, and Harbor View autos make frequent trips
at special low fares.

A Wilderness Camp at Sixth Lake
has been cleared, and a large, substantial 2-room cabin erected, with separate
cabin for guides—the property of Harbor View. It is easy of access, though
remote from signs of civilization, and
the surroundings are beautiful. Sixth
Lake is part of a 40-mile chain of lovely
lakes and streams, in the midst of a
great moose country, with lively fishing
all around. Ladies will find life at this
camp, with its home-like comforts, a
novel and delightful experience. A five-
day trip from Harbor View for two people need not cost more than $75, cover-
ing auto hire, guide, canoe, fishing
license, all food supplies, and use of
both cabins—everything except person-
al equipment.

> You may leave Boston after lunch,
> and have your own trout for supper
> next evening at this camp.

Vacations and leisure

Up until the late 1800s, all men, except nobility and a handful of the privileged few, were expected to work six days a week, 52 weeks a year. Up until the late 1930s, even white-collar types who commuted to Wall Street worked five and a half days a week. The summer vacation, like swimming, sun bathing and picnicking on a sandy beach, was not yet dreamed of by the common unliberated man. Certainly a paid vacation was unheard of.

When summertime began to signal vacation time, a whole new industry and concept of living came into being. The summer hotel was invented and sprang up in all kinds of bucolic, woodland, mountainous, seaside and maritime locations across Europe and North America. Natural beauty, open spaces, freedom to move about, sunshine, relaxation and fresh air were what people wanted —and bought.

The vacation movement began with the more affluent and quickly trickled down to nearly everybody. The first "guests" at Harbor View were relatively wealthy, or were in the teaching business and had obligatory summer vacations.

The existence of the country hotel, boarding house and resort came under pressure in the 1930s because of the worldwide depression. During the Great Depression, I remember, many of my schoolmates told about going to their grand-parents' farms for their vacations. Many resorts that did not close their doors by 1950 have done so subsequently.

Among the survivors are those that changed with the times. Most of these cater to special-target clientele, such as bus tours, conventions, honeymooners and those who are willing to pay for nostalgia.

The former Annex, now the Hotel, around 1946. The dining wing is on the right.

Harbourview Inn in 1993. Most of the verandah enclosed.

Harbour View does not fit into any such category. The motel, the private second home, luxury cruises, package tours, campers and mobile homes have absorbed the trade that was formerly enjoyed by the old-time country hotel and cabin colony. Minimum wage laws dealt the death blow to those that were only barely surviving before these laws were passed.

Harbor View House and Cottages was highly successful under William Cossaboom, its founder, because he had hold of the right thing at the right time. If he had not died prematurely, and before the crash of 1929, and if World War II had not practically shut the place down, he would have run into the same financial problems his sons experienced later on. But with his expertise and with the self-discipline common to founders of all successful enterprises, he might have reacted differently.

The debts run up by the Cossaboom sons forced Arthur Jefferson of Bear River to call in his loans to Harbor View and resulted in his assuming full ownership in 1947. Not wanting to be in the hotel business, Jefferson was relieved to sell the enterprise in the same year to Walter Flett of Halifax.

Flett built a concrete swimming pool, eliminated the boardwalk and changed the spelling from Harbor to "Harbour," but made few other changes at Harbour View. He also made few repairs. His hard-working manager, Charlie Longmire of Bridgetown, was constantly in motion overseeing everything. Gene Ford, his assistant, handled entertainment, including the running of dances, bingo games and special events at the casino.

Harbour View House was closed for the first summer ever in 1942 because of World War II. Gasoline rationing and the unavailability of staff were the main reasons. The Pines Hotel remained closed, too. In 1943 the hotel was still closed, but water and electricity were on to serve the navy families that were living in cottages rented from the hotel. HMCS Cornwallis in Deep Brook was then in operation, training recruits for the navy.

My parents managed to be here for ten days, nevertheless, but there were no meals served at the hotel. They were back again in 1944 for a week, as was Mrs. Witherbee, Mr. Witherbee having died the preceding winter. The Fords were here and so were the McLennans, the new owners of the Lord cottage (#18).

My parents were here August 1945, on the day the war ended, and watched the star shells, rockets and flares over HMCS Cornwallis light up the whole Basin to celebrate that happy event.

By 1952 cottage ownership had dwindled to only seven: Barrie, Fries, Kinsolving, Mathers, Odell, Shenstone and Turnbull. The Cossaboom daughters had married or moved away: Lillian (Mrs. Ralph) Sheppard of Hartford, Connecticut; Winnie (Mrs. A. C.) McIntyre of Rockport, Massachusetts; Nellie (Mrs. Joseph) Steadman of Smith's Cove; and Florence, a school-teacher in New Germany, NS.

Aside from changes of faces, families and buildings, there has been a marked change in the appearance and ambience of Harbour View because of the growth of vegetation. Argonaut Knoll and Harbor View were built on open farmland, mostly meadows and pastures. Photographs of those early days are remarkable, primarily because of this openness and the magnificent panorama seen from all cottages.

In fact, this was true of most of Smith's Cove then, because it was a community of small general farms. Oxen and horses pulled plows, wagons and other farm equipment, and these animals required hay and pasture. Every house in the village of Smith's Cove, farm or not, had at least a one-cow barn and at least one cow pasturing on Sunset Hill (Hardscrabble).

When the Cossaboom family and Walter Flett ran Harbour View, they owned all the land. Cottage owners merely leased their lots from them. As most of the land was still used for farming or gardening, it was necessary to keep the fields open and keep trees to a minimum.

From the time that lots were bought by private individuals (after 1967) some owners chose to allow trees and other natural vegetation to grow up. Other trees, such as poplar and red pine, were planted and have grown vigorously. This has chopped up the wide panorama into narrower views.

The former openness permitted expansive views in all directions from every point in the village, including Harbour View, diminished not one bit the brilliant sunshine, and enhanced the feeling of a friendly, close-knit community. Verandahs furnished enough shade and most houses had one. All Harbor View buildings had them except the barn, garages and pump house.

This openness and feeling of large common space have been largely preserved in the area extending northeast from Harbour View Road, including the tennis court and the first five cottages

(14, 16, 18, 20, and 22). In 1993 the owners of those five cottages took the additional step of buying, in common, the meadow in front of them that extends down to the mean high tide line, thus preserving that much of the original Harbor View atmosphere as well as their view the Basin.

Elsewhere the planting and growth of trees has made many cottages more secluded. While the trees increase the feeling of privacy, they also screen views previously enjoyed from other cottages. Neighbors were thus unthinkingly deprived of views, light and circulation of air.

For those of us who prefer openness and expansive views it is a fight to keep the forest from swallowing us up. Nothing disappears faster than an open field that is neglected. Soon the view across it also disappears.

Along with trees, especially cone-bearing ones, come red squirrels. Although winsome beggars they may appear, they can cause much damage and nuisance if they gain access to a cottage. Trees, especially spruce, close to a cottage can be an invitation to damage by squirrels and by storm-lashed branches scrubbing against the roof or siding shingles.

Before we cut down the spruce trees to the south of Sunnymeade, the squirrels used the roof ridge as a thoroughfare. This resulted in their tiny feet wearing clear through the many layers of asphalt shingles along the ridge.

In July 1996 all the trees between cottages #22 and #24 were removed and replaced by a few shrubs. This action reduced the hazard of fire, squirrels and windfall; expanded the views from the road and from both cottages; increased the light and airiness of both cottages; and decreased the dampness.

As was true everywhere, World War II brought inflation. The price of a cord of split, seasoned hardwood in Smith's Cove jumped to $18. (It kept on going up and reached $60 in 1980, $80 in 1983 and $120 in 1993.)

The first quarter century

Dr. Allen Shenstone was here in the early summers of this century and has recorded details about this family summer camp. As one who was born in 1893, graduated from college in 1909 and was a regular summer resident up until his death in 1980, he experienced Harbour View over a longer period than anyone else. His account of the early days is the only reliable one. Here it is:

> When it opened, the hotel included a main building in which there were bedrooms, bathrooms, a sitting room, dining room and kitchen, and four small cabins. None of the four original cabins (6, 7, 8 and 10) had toilet facilities. Two of them (6 and 7) were divided by a central partition into two bedrooms. They were made with whole horizontal logs caulked with moss. The writer spent his first night in Smith's Cove in 1903 in cabin 6.
>
> The casino in position 22 probably was in existence very early in the century. It was built of whole logs in the vertical position, a method of construction that was popular for a number of years. [It is David Irvine's observation that those vertical logs were actually sawn in half lengthwise. The joints of the flat sides on the interior were then covered with battens. Some of these walls are still in existence.]
>
> Mr. John B. Lord, who had for some years been spending the summers at Deep Brook in the house of John Purdy, the boat builder, built cabin 18 about 1901 on land leased from Mr. Cossaboom. He was an enthusiastic sailor and had had built for his son, Bright Lord, a small sailboat, the Yankee Doodle, that was so well built [and maintained] that it was still sound when last seen by the writer in 1957.
>
> About 1902, cabins 16, 30, 32 and 34 were built by a group of Boston friends: Mr. Kaunt, Mr. Ray Shipman Vi Frank B. Witherbee and Mr. Dodd. A little later Mr Chase

built 45 and 47 for rent. Number 43, known as Knoll Top, a double-decker with bedrooms for rent and a central sitting room, and 49, the Twin cottage, were built not long after.

By 1921 cottages 16, 17, 18, 20, 24, 26, 28, 36 and 48 had been built on Cossaboom property and 50 on land purchased from Bishop Jaggar by Mr. Ford. My recollection is that 14, 15, 19, 40, 42, and 44 were built later, as certainly were 27 and the chapel.

The chapel was built by subscription on land donated by Mr. Cossaboom. The presence of Bishop Richardson and the religious devotion of Miss Ogden were largely responsible for its construction. In the twenties and thirties the congregation was so large that it often necessitated chairs in the aisle and outside the entrance door.

At one time there was a road to the beach below #44 and a large boat house with a slip reaching to low-water mark. The remains of the slip are still visible. The boathouse was destroyed by a storm before 1931, but the foundation timbers are, however, still visible.

The slip at #53 was built during the First World War and was abandoned shortly after. The main hotel slip was always maintained at the foot of the road from the hotel to the beach.

In the years before the First World War the cove harboured a considerable fleet of sailboats, including two large ones belonging to Mr. Shipman and Mr. Lord, and seven identical 18-foot sailing dories for racing.

Robert Milbank writes of these boats as follows:

My father bought one of these from Mr. Shipman about 1902. She was named *OO-AAH*. During the winter we stored her in Deep Brook with Captain John Purdy, the boat-builder. He described her as a gaff-rigged Swampscott dory with a narrow, flat bottom and a centreboard. When I asked what her over-all length was, he replied, 'The plans called for 17 feet, but some's 16 and some's 18. It's just the way the wood bent."

Shenstone continues:

There were also a number of other sailboats of various sorts, including our own, which was considered by the local sailors as too radical a design. It was later owned by Charles Turnbull and then Kelsey Raymond.

There being no motor boats until shortly before the war [World War I] and no motor cars, the easiest way to go to Digby was by sailboat. This was usually much quicker than by driving a horse and carriage.

The hotel provided fine large buckboards for picnics, etc., and excellent horses. In fact Mr. Cossaboom did a great deal of horse trading in the winter as a regular occupation.

Arrival at the hotel was usually by train at what was originally called 'Panorama Platform' and later 'Imbertville Station.' The ship from Saint John was the *Prince Rupert* and on the Boston-Yarmouth run were the *Prince George* and the *Boston*.

The chief amusement was sailing and the Basin was always alive with boats. The Digby waterfront was so full of boats and moorings that it was difficult to sail into the harbour without fouling some obstacle.

Other amusements at Harbour View were picnics, tennis, quoits and lawn bowling. The first tennis court was on the level green above the present pool. A second court was built above it and is the existing court. Later the lower one was converted to croquet. Mr. Roome maintained a private green behind his cabin.

Tennis was very popular, the courts being in constant use, and tournaments and matches were held with such places as Lour Lodge, the most fashionable hotel in Digby.

At the turn of the century Charles F. Chase of New Jersey, who had admired the Harbor View property while staying across the mouth of the Bear River at the Colonial Arms Hotel, leased open farm land farther out on Harbor View point from Cossaboom and began a summer family camp. Cabins numbered 41, 43, 45 and 47 on D. L. Turner's map of 1931 comprised the Argonaut Knoll Camp. Guests at Argonaut Knoll took their meals at the Harbor View House.

Argonaut Knoll

After World War I, Chase sold his Argonaut Knoll to Cossaboom and it was merged into the Harbor View House and Cottages operation. The Chases remained steady summer people and ardent supporters of the community's religious life.

Shenstone continues:

> By 1931, when Dr. Turner's map was made, the whole complex had reached full development. Mr. Cossaboom had bought out Mr. Chase about 1918 and all the cottages except 41, 43, and 49 were privately owned. Many had gone through a number of hands as is shown on the attached list.
>
> During the thirties, the motor car began to change the former idea of a summer resort, and the cabins gradually fell into possession of the hotel as the older people no longer came and the younger ones preferred more and more to move about rather than spend the whole summer in one place. Cabins became dilapidated and were torn down, or repaired and modernized so that their present state is in many cases very unlike the original appearance. Logs were frequently replaced by slabs and later by siding or shingles.
>
> The original very primitive toilet facilities have been replaced by services requiring larger quantities of water than when everyone was supplied from three wells pumped by windmills. When the wind failed, drinking water was drawn from the 'Sulis Spring,' which was near the shore below cabin 48.
>
> Candles and oil lamps were first replaced by local direct current battery and generator systems which eventually

gave way to the present public [electric power] distribution.

In 1909 the present hotel [now Harbourview Inn] was built to provide more rooms for visitors who did not want the larger expense of a cabin, and in 1923 the house opposite it was built to accommodate Mrs. Cossaboom and her family of eight children.

The original hotel was destroyed by fire, which broke out in the attic during the lunch hour. The cause was almost certainly the deterioration of the upper part of the main fireplace chimney. The steps at the end of the present dining room were in an exactly similar position on the old hotel[1].

Bear Island had a house on it and a large dock.

Peacocks were kept on the island up to about 1905. There was also a fish smoke house on the southern end. At normal high tides the island was continuous, but at spring tides the smoke house formed a separate small island. Only at the lows of the spring tides was it possible to walk to the island, so it is obvious that the bar is rising steadily.

The house on Bear Island

Smoking of fish, especially herring, had evidently been a large industry before 1900. The shores of the Basin were

---

1   The steps were, in fact, the original steps, having been one of the few bits of the hotel that were not destroyed by the fire. They have since then been moved and then replaced altogether.

lined with smoke houses, there being a [smoke] house to about every mile of shore.

The Pines existed as a small hotel [before the First World War],

Lobster parties in the summer were illegal, there being no pounds, but there were various houses that would provide 'chicken dinners.'

A buckboard or covered carriage made regular trips to take visitors to meals, especially on rainy days.

Dr. Shenstone makes a cryptic note of a drowning (Cossitt) that took place in 1905. He tells of evening walks up Hardscrabble to watch the sunset. I took that walk many times, but now there are so many trees that there is no view from there at all. The old photographs in the Smith's Cove Museum show how open that hill was up until World War II.

The hotel was originally lit by kerosene lamps and candles. Kerosene was called "coal oil" then because originally it was produced by the distillation of cannel coal, a more costly process than the present method of distilling it from petroleum. Then Cossaboom installed acetylene lights for a short time because they were brighter and more modern.

Around 1920 he switched to electricity by installing a Delco generator in one end of the pump house. When electric power became available from the utility company, he switched to it.

The second quarter century

The hotel was run by William M. Cossaboom until his death in 1927 at age 54. He had been a strong advocate of the development of hydroelectric power in Nova Scotia. He had built the hotel into a sizeable operation worth, according to his obituary, more than $200,000, and with a dining room that could accommodate 200 guests.

The hotel provided guides and outfitted parties for hunting and fishing trips to its camp on Sixth Lake. To reach this backwoods facility one crossed Lake Jolly by canoe, having put in at the clothes pin factory (long since gone) at the end of the road. The traveler then paddled up the long winding inlet, portaged across into Ninth Lake, paddled across it, portaged across to Eighth Lake, paddled across it, portaged to Seventh Lake, paddled across it and finally portaged over to Sixth Lake. All except the first portage are short and easy carries.

Bedding, in the form of blanket rolls, food and other gear in sturdy Mi'kmaq pack baskets, and the canoe were all carried by the guides. The sports were encumbered only by their fishing or hunting gear.

Ownership of this two-room Sixth Lake camp came into the hands of Ralph Cossitt in part payment for what was owed him by Harbor View when the wartime financial pinch became severe. I first went back there after World War II with my younger brother, Bob. We went for three days and did not take a guide. We caught no fish. The camp was on a narrow point of land and commanded the lake. The remains of the chimney can still be seen there.

Meals in the old hotel's dining room were legendary. Each one was announced by the ringing of a large hand bell at both the front door and the back. The bell was too heavy for me to ring my first summer, but later it was often my privilege to be allowed to ring it, and of course to be the first one into the dining room.

But that never did me any good. It was unthinkable that I should be seated, let alone eat, before the adults in my family. Children were definitely second-class citizens.

That first summer at age three I had to have all meals in the children's dining room with the other little children, the chauffeurs and the nursemaids (they were not called sitters or au pairs then). Eating in the children's dining room had its good points, though, chief of which was that we did not have sit around and squirm for a long time while there was a lot of inane and uninteresting grown-up conversation.

New menus were printed fresh every day and for each meal—breakfast, dinner and supper. They were printed on a hand-cranked printing press with movable lead type that slid into tracks on a revolving drum. This press and the type for it are still stored in the barn.

Dinner was always at mid-day, the old-fashioned way. When I was learning to read, my family had to suffer through my reading the entire menu aloud at each meal. Once all eyes popped when I pronounced "Chinese oatmeal" instead of cheese omelet. Many years later (1953) my cousin Wallace did the same thing with "Rolled Cats" and "Roast Lion" (rolled oats and roast loin.)

The menus were printed on a high grade of light tag stock that was perfect for folding and making all sorts of origami-style things, especially boxes and cootie catchers.

Robert Milbank preserved a 1935 menu with Murray Oickle's blueberry pie recipe scrawled on the back. The menu and recipe are reproduced on the next two pages to stimulate the reader's appetite.

HARBOR VIEW HOUSE
SMITH'S COVE

SUPPER

Corn Chowder

Fried Fresh Haddock

Cold Boiled Ham	Cold Boiled Tongue	Cold Roast Veal
Cold Roast Pork	Cold Roast Lamb	Cold Roast Beef

COOKED TO ORDER
Broiled Sirloin Steak

Baked Pork Sausage   Broiled Pork Chops

Broiled Lamb Chops   Broiled Ham   Broiled Veal Chops

Fried Scrambled Boiled and Poached Eggs

Fruit Salad

Spaghetti Italian   Lobster a la Newburg   Cheese Omelet

Cream of Tomatoes

Virginia Corn Cake

Orange Pineapple Ice Cream   Chocolate Ice Cream

Bueberries with Cream

Green Apple Sauce   Preserved Peaches

Lemon Jelly with Whipped Cream

Baked Custard

Ginger Snaps   Orange Layer Cake   Drop Cookies

Cream Soda Crackers with Canadian or Kraft Cheese

Wheat Bread   Graham Bread

Tea   Coffee   Cocoa   Postum   Milk

HOURS FOR MEALS

Breakfast 8 to 9   Dinner 12.30 to 1.30   Supper 6 to 7

SUNDAY

Breakfast 8.30 to 9 30   Dinner 1 to 2   Supper 6 to 7

Guests having meals sent to the cabins will kindly furnish their own
dishes and baskets. Extra charge for all meals served outside the Dining Room.

Sunday September 1 1935

Blueberry Pie
1½ cups flour
1 " shortening (butter &...
pinch of salt
moisten with ice
cold water

blueberries
1½ cups sugar (lots of
butter)
cook until done
½ cup of cold water.

Violet A. Faulkenham
Murray Oickle.

Harbor View House

Murray Oickle's blueberry pie recipe. Violet Faulkenham from Lunenburg was head waitress for many years.

The meals were beautifully prepared and presented in dozens and dozens of small individual dishes, which meant big, heavy trays for the waitresses and thoroughly cluttered tables. The tables were spread with white linen tablecloths and each person had a fresh white linen napkin every day. The waitresses wore traditional white-and-gray uniforms that included aprons and caps.

The food was cooked simply in the old-fashioned country style —lots of roasts, fried and boiled things and the best desserts in the world, such as pies, puddings and homemade ice cream. There was no limit to how much one could eat and multiple desserts were not uncommon.

Murray Oickle was a wonderful chef and was always obliging and never flustered. If we brought in a dozen or so freshly-caught flounder, he took it in his stride and saw that "fresh fried or broiled filet of sole" was available for supper that evening. Harbour View was fortunate to have Murray as chef for a great many years.

Meals were social events, too. Because everybody was required to have all meals at the hotel, everybody saw and talked with everybody else. Everybody was also seen by everybody else, and that meant we were constantly changing our clothes for meals. Men had to wear ties and jackets for Sunday dinner and every evening for supper. Imagine the complicated wardrobe changes required simply by digging clams in the morning and having a swim in the early afternoon—a minimum of six changes; count them.

Because of all the changes of clothes, no one traveled light. Each person brought along a trunk—a wardrobe trunk for each grown-up, a steamer trunk for each child and nursemaid. In those days it was simple and cheap to bring or ship a trunk. It was usually just checked on one's ticket and there was no extra charge for it. Kelsey Raymond remembers coming alone with his steamer trunk from New York during the Depression and staying all summer at his grandmother's house in Smith's Cove.

But travel was not the casual thing it is today. One dressed to travel as though going to a formal occasion in New York. Men and boys wore suits, ties and polished leather shoes. Travel by car also meant the likelihood of having a flat tire, and time had to be allowed to change tires, especially when going to catch the steamer at Yarmouth.

In 1927, after William Cossaboom, a diabetic, died at age 54, Earl, the eldest of the four Cossaboom sons and who loved to cook, briefly took over the management job. People then whispered that he was a "bad one," but the only reason for this that I could ever find was that he married four times.

This clashed with the then prevailing strong Victorian sense of what was proper. Back then, people were close-mouthed about many topics that smacked of scandal. The rule was, "If you can't say anything good about a person, then keep quiet."

At any rate, Earl did not run Harbor View long, but turned the reins over to his next-oldest brother, Douglas ("Duke"), who was born in 1907. Earl moved to Bouckville near Cazanovia, New York. There he acquired and ran his own hotel, Cossaboom's Hotel.

None of the four Cossaboom sisters—Lillian, Winifred ("Winnie"), Nellie and Florence—ever ran the hotel, but they all worked in it at times in lesser capacities.

Clara Cossaboom, William's widow, owned Harbor View from 1928 to 1933, but Earl ran it from 1928 up to 1934. Clara died in 1960 at age 91.

Douglas ran it from 1934 to 1940. Mary ("Mamie"), Douglas's wife, took over for the war years of 1940 to 1943. Gordon, 1943 to 1947. Walter Flett 1947 to 1967.

Donald Cossaboom, the youngest son, never ran the hotel. Douglas was a keen tennis player and spent much time on the clay court, which he always had carefully maintained.

Tennis was an important activity at Harbor View in the Cossaboom era. It got more attention before 1938 than afterwards, because the hotel's spacious side verandah, with its long row of rocking chairs overlooking the court, was popular as a spectator gallery. The rocking chairs were often filled with knitters, talkers and readers when there was no tennis in progress. Little kids were not welcome there.

Male tennis players wore long white trousers, either white flannel or white duck; white shirts; white socks and white sneakers. The ladies also wore only white skirts, not slacks or shorts.

There were two telephones at Harbor View, both of them in the hotel office. One was connected to the Digby switchboard, the other to Bear River. (There was some idle speculation then as to whether Digby or Bear River would grow to be the more important town.) Both phones were on party lines and the calling was done by turning the magneto crank after listening to be sure there was no one already on the line. An incoming call for a guest was a major event and a car was sent to bring the guest back to the phone.

Beyond the tennis court toward the Basin was the bowling green. Its grass was kept clipped close and carefully rolled. This was a very dressy sport. Men removed their jackets, but kept their ties on. Often they wore straw hats; the skimmer or boater style was most popular.

This was the true game of English lawn bowling, played with a small china ball, the jack, that was first thrown down the green, and with large black balls weighted on one side so that they traveled a curved course and could be made to sneak around behind another player's ball without touching it, and thus get closer to the jack and yet enjoy the protection of the opponent's ball. My mother excelled at bowling, but it taxed my father's patience and he declined to play, preferring tennis.

The present lounging area between the tennis court and the pool is where the bowling green was. It is there now that the Cottagers' Association members hold their annual picnic. There was no swimming pool there then.

To the north of the tennis court, in front of what is now the Clapps' cottage, was the croquet court. The ground is still level there and is graded for croquet, but is too rough for that game now.

The barn behind the frog pond was a favorite for all the children. Its loft was full of hay, not in bales, but "long hay" pitched up there by fork from the horse-drawn hay wagon in the center bay. That hay was for hiding and jumping and dreaming. It was also used to feed the horses and the four or five cows that were housed down below.

Bob Milbank and I both learned how to milk there. He reminded me of the wonderful sound made by the first few hard squirts hitting the bottom of the pail.

Behind the barn was the pig pen and manure pile. Slops from the hotel were fed to the pigs. The pigs and manure lay to the southeast of our first cottage (#6), so we were seldom bothered by the smell, but window screens, fly paper and fly swatters helped keep things under control indoors. When we became aware of the odor, it was a reliable indication that rain was on the way.

The old pig pen was removed and now serves David and Sylvia Irvine as their garden shed.

A popular outing in those days was a lobster feed at Casey's Fundy View House. By prearrangement, Mr. Casey would pick up several carloads of Harbor View people at the Government Wharf in Digby and transport them in his large, open motor boat to the wharf at Victoria Beach. The party would there divide into two groups; one walked, the other was driven to the hotel. There was always a cottage on the grounds where the guests could open their own bottles and their pour their own before-dinner drinks.

The boat ride back to Digby was a special treat on a clear, star-studded night.

Head south on St. George Street in Annapolis Royal, pass the cemetery, go up the hill, and at the top on the right you will find a private home that in the twenties and thirties used to be the Wishing Rock Tea Room[2]. Having afternoon tea there with plenty of sweet cakes and cookies was a pleasant treat. The place got its name from a rounded boulder embedded in the lawn. A silent wish made when standing on top of the rock was sure to be granted.

Another, but longer and more adventurous, outing was a drive to "Kedgie" (Lake Kejimkujik). By the landing at the end of the road, in a box nailed to a tree, was a telephone with a crank on it. A call on it summoned a motor launch that carried passengers to the lodge for midday dinner. The lodge is long since gone and the lake and surrounding area is now a world-class national park.

Board at Harbor View in 1932 (per week, with three full meals a day) for those in privately owned cottages was: 2 adults $42, nurse $14, child $7, chauffeur $25 (including his room as well as his board.) Bob Milbank remembers his mother saying that board was $7 a week per person when she first came to Harbor View in 1910. The U.S. dollar was worth C$1.21 in the spring of 1934 and C$1.15 in June. In 1934 the weekly board (no room) per person was $17.50. The trend was clearly deflationary.

Bob Milbank reminisces about travel to Nova Scotia as follows:

> My first trip was in 1913 when I was 9 months old. I slept in an upper berth [in a train from Boston to Saint John, having traveled the entire distance from New Jersey by rail] with Steffy, our Polish maid.
>
> We went many different ways. Several years we took the Fall River boat from New York to Fall River, Massachusetts, and the train from there (50 miles) to Boston. Sometime after the Cape Cod Canal was opened we took the SS[3] *Boston* or the *SS New York* from New York to Boston. From there we took the *SS Prince Arthur* or the *SS Prince George* to Yarmouth.

---

2   The house and tea room, after years of standing empty, were taken down in 2024.

3   SS, meaning Steam Ship, is not used on today's ships. Being powered by diesel engines, their names are prefixed by MV—Motor Vessel.

After visiting Mr. Ross's store in Yarmouth to check out the Yeager and other English woolens, we went the final leg of the journey to Imbertville Station by train.

Eventually, the two Princes were replaced by the *SS Evangeline* and the *SS Yarmouth*, larger and more seaworthy ships of the Eastern Steamship Company.

After we started to take our own car, we could take longer to shop in Yarmouth and to stop for lobster lunch at the Riverside Inn in Meteghan River.

Still later, the Eastern Steamship Company added the larger *SS Acadia* and *SS Nova Scotia* for the direct New York to Yarmouth run. This meant sailing from New York around noon, cruising up Long Island Sound and waking up the next morning in Yarmouth—a delightful experience.

At first glance—a flashback

Although my three-year-old mind didn't understand it, it seemed shameful to treat Nanny's black Buick that way. Men drained out all the gasoline and then they pushed the big four-door beauty with jumpseats and running boards, with trunk and spare tire behind, onto a cargo net spread out on the wharf. Ropes with big hooks were attached to the net.

One man waved his hand and the four ropes pulled the corners of the net up, trapping the car like a wild animal. The car rose slowly in the air, paused, swung over the open deck hatch of the *SS Nerissa* and just as slowly sank out of sight into the ship's hold.

I was three years old and my brother Billy was only a two-month-old baby. The year was 1926. This was our first trip to Nova Scotia.

The *Nerissa*, a coal burning steamer of the now-defunct White Cross Line—white X on a black funnel—wasn't large or fast, but she seemed enormous to me. The whistle was very big and terrifying, and catapulted me shrieking to my mother when it first sounded.

Everything was bustle and confusion before the lines were cast off. An important man in a white jacket walked around striking a gong of some kind and calling loudly, "All ashore that's goin' ashore."

My father, who was constrained by the niggardly two-week vacation that Wood Gundy & Company allowed at that time, stood on the wharf waving at us. He had to remain in New York. To me it looked as though he was standing on some kind of lower deck. I knew he couldn't come with us and this was my only sadness that day.

It wasn't until the ship began to move that I realized he was not on the ship at all. I had been screaming, "Daddy, get off the ship," to the amusement of all who heard me.

Once away from the wharf, the ship instantly became smaller

and there was no more bustle.

There were deck chairs and the women sat in them wrapped in blankets. I found it unbearable to sit still. I only wanted to run around the ship.

After a while, probably after leaving the protected waters of Long Island Sound, my mother and Nellie, who wore a white uniform and took care of Billy, became seasick and suffered terribly for the remainder of the voyage. Nanny, my grandmother Caroline Hanson, and I never felt a twinge. We were in the *Nerissa* for two days and two nights before reaching Halifax.

I have the impression that I made many friends on that trip, but the only ones I remember were two stewards in white jackets. They were very important people and could take me where passengers were not allowed. Beyond those doors there were big pots and shiny kettles and all kinds of things that I had never seen before.

Best of all, they fed me dates. Dates were beyond doubt the best and yummiest things I had ever tasted.

There was a marvelous wide door down there in that forbidden realm. It reached from floor to ceiling and was wide open to the ocean except for a rope across the middle. It was exciting to stand there just above the water and look out and up, to see broad swells rolling toward the ship, and then magically disappear as the ship rolled and rose up their faces.

My new friends were perfect hosts and very attentive. They never let me out of their sight and one of them held my hand while I stood looking out that wonderful door.

When they returned me to the other world, that of passengers and other mortals, my devastated mother knelt and crushed me with hugs and kisses. It was embarrassing even at the age of three. She and Nellie had been miserable in their staterooms. (Seasickness can make saints, sinners and heroes whimper and hope to die, but I didn't know anything about that then.)

Both she and Nellie must have thought the other, or maybe Nanny, had charge of me. Nanny must have been deep into a good book in her deck chair. Surely, Charles had climbed up the rail and fallen overboard.

The rest of that trip must have been pretty dull because I remember nothing about it except that I climbed a ladder to get into my bunk and that the stateroom window was round.

Nanny was born in Gardiner, Maine. As a young woman she went to New York "to teach the deaf" and ended up marrying my grandfather. From then on she lived in East Orange, New Jersey, but never reconciled herself to the suffocating heat and humidity of metropolitan summers.

My father, who was born in Saint John, New Brunswick, the original air-conditioned city, and grew up in nearby Rothesay, suggested that she visit Nova Scotia, where the summer weather would suit her better. His grand-mother, a very strict, Biblish woman who had blue lips and never smiled, summered at the Sea Breeze Hotel in Deep Brook. She rented a cabin there, one in a row of small, box-like cells that faced the Annapolis Basin across a high meadow.

The meadow is still there on the water side of Route 1 to the west of Cornwallis, but mercifully the cabins are gone. The hotel, now a private home, and the well with its own roof look much as they did in the twenties and thirties. Water cranked up the well was dumped into a chute built into the well house wall and ran out into a pail waiting on the ground outside.

Each Sea Breeze cabin had a curtain across one corner to serve as a place to hang clothes. There was no running water and no plumbing. Each cabin had a wash stand with basin and large white china pitcher, and an enamel pail with lid underneath for dirty water. Under the bed was a crockery chamber pot with lid.

String hammocks were hung between the cabins and were used for the afternoon siesta. (The hammocks and the well windlass were the only things I liked about that place, and hammocks were definitely not for my siestas.)

Nanny was delighted with the climate and the area, but could not bear to stay long in one of those Spartan boxes. Looking around for something better, she soon found Harbor View House and Cottages, and she moved there. She arranged to bring us there the following summer (1926).

My next recollection is that of our first cabin at Smith's Cove. It was #6, the one at the corner of Harbour View Road and Beachcomber Lane, then called Harbor View Road and Shore Road. Later, that building was called the Brown cabin, referring to the name of its occupants, not its color.

In 1926 it had a permanently-screened sleeping porch attached to the side nearest the casino, the building now known as Cossaboom Corner. The sleeping porch was only large enough for one single bed. It was there that Billy took his naps which, it seemed, was most of the time. "Be quiet! Don't wake Billy."

The cabin—they were all called cabins then, no matter how large—was directly across the circle from the hotel, and was the first in a row of three. Miss Barnum stayed in the middle one. It was the size of a one-car garage and I could jump from our porch to hers.

I loved our first little cabin (#6), and I saw a lot of the inside of it that summer because it rained for fourteen days straight. We had basins and pails everywhere to catch the drips from the ancient roof. My bed had an umbrella tied over its head and a poncho draped over the foot.

At her wit's end after a few wet days, my mother borrowed an old balance scale from Dr. Campbell of Bear River and I set about weighing mounds of sawdust into all sorts of containers.

The pond behind our cabin that first year was the home of a band of melodious frogs. They kept Nanny awake with their symphonies and conversations, but I loved them. My father tried to catch them using his bamboo fly rod and a red fly. (By 1967 this pond had silted in and had become no more than a swampy area with a stream running through it. David Irvine dug it out again.)

In the middle of the circle between our cabin and the hotel was a cherry tree. With a little help I could get to the lowest branch and remain quiet, content and in a known location for a long time.

In that tree I learned to climb, and I scrambled all over it. The dark, ripe cherries were packed with juice that stained conspicuously. After my first trip up the tree wearing white linen shorts, white cotton shirt and white socks I heard quite a bit about those stains.

The American spelling, "Harbor," was used in those days. It wasn't until after World War II that the Canadian/British spelling, "Harbour," was adopted. Still later, when the Irvines sold the hotel to the Webbs, without any fanfare the more space-age "Harbourview" came into use for the renamed Harbourview Inn, and then, later, for Harbourview Cottagers Association.

It's still the same dear place that keeps on evolving as the years and fashions change, and as the economy of the times and the aging and frailties of its denizens dictate.

Our second trip to Smith's Cove was on the Eastern Steamship Lines' *SS Evangeline* from New York to Yarmouth. The trip took only 24 hours.

For many years we came on that same run, but some trips were on her sister ship, the *SS Saint John*. Later the line ran the larger *SS Acadia* on the New York run. They also ran service between Boston and Yarmouth, only an overnight run.

In 1924 the *SS Northland* of the Boston-Yarmouth Line made the run from Boston. She had 230 staterooms and could carry 30 automobiles—16 hours each way.

The 1924 overland alternative was to go by train from North Station, Boston, to Saint John, an overnight trip, and take the *SS Empress* across to Digby (three hours). The *Empress* (1916-1930) carried only 16 cars.

The aged *Empress* was replaced by the sprightly *SS Princess Helene*. The *Princess Helene* was replaced in 1963 by the first *MV Princess of Acadia*. In 1971 she, in turn, was replaced by the present *MV Princess of Acadia*, and CN Marine built her a new terminal out in the Gut, just a little closer to Saint John and away from the congestion of Digby harbour.

In 1997 CN Marine, a crown corporation, sold its service, vessels and facilities for the Digby-Saint John and the Yarmouth-Bar Harbor runs to Northumberland Ferries, Ltd., the company that provided ferry service to Prince Edward Island. (The new bridge link to that province makes ferries there unnecessary.) They plan to consolidate the Bay of Fundy service to run between both Bar Harbor and Saint John from the deep water terminal in Digby Gut. They also plan eventually to replace the *Princess of Acadia* with a modern, high-speed, twin-hull vessel. These changes may take several years to complete.

To keep things in perspective, no one drove from Boston to Saint John before World War II. The trip from Boston to Yarmouth by air in 1956 took 1-1/2 hours, but very few people flew then. Air travelers now often rent cars at the airport for their stay in Nova Scotia. Present-day highways make driving time from Boston to Saint John an easy eight hours or a tiring 12 hours from New York.

Local colour

From the rear of the hotel a narrow boardwalk ran along the right side of the gravel road up past our cottage (Nanny's #22). Another one began across the road and continued up the hill. Some over-weight adult was constantly breaking through a weak board and "Mac" McGuiness was repeatedly being summoned to replace it. There were electric street lights along the boardwalk.

The street lights continued to operate long after the boardwalk had been torn up. In the 1970s the telephone company, on whose poles the lights were mounted, forced the removal of the lights and their wiring.

Mac was a scrawny, silent man in overalls and railroad engin-eer's cap. He was silent because he seemed always to have his mouth full of tobacco. A thin trickle of brown juice ran down a groove in his weather-beaten face from the corner of his mouth to under his chin.

Mac did all the odd jobs around the hotel. More importantly, he was the Pied Piper to us children because he drove a strange little truck around the grounds and allowed us to either hang on the running boards or pile into the back. He operated the pump that forced water up into a large water tower over the pump house. He knew it was full when it overflowed.

The metal parts of Mac's truck were unwashed black and the wooden ones were dusty, dull red, except for the floorboards which may never have had any finish on them at all. There was a roof of wooden slats covered with heavy, black waterproof fabric, as was common before integral sheet steel roofs were introduced. The roof covered the cab and bed as well, but the sides and rear were wide open.

The engine started easily with a crank. I know because I started it one Sunday afternoon (Mac's only day off) and drove it just far enough to ruin a front tire. Barbara Bull was with me and we shared the cost of a new tire, and went without candy for the rest of the summer. Barbara had a broken front tooth that made her look fearless and adventuresome.

Mac cut ice in the winter from the square pond behind the chapel and packed it away in sawdust in the ice house beside the pond. He delivered ice every morning to the hotel and all the cottages that ordered it.

At each cottage he washed the cake of ice and cut it down to fit precisely into each icebox. The ice went into the upper compartment and the chilled air flowed down by convection to the lower compartment. There was a copper funnel under our icebox to lead the melt water neatly out through a hole in the floor.

Mac cut, split, delivered and stacked firewood. He was constantly in motion and never smiled.

The pond was used for ice up through the winter of 1968. That year David Irvine cut the ice with a chain saw instead of the traditional old hand saw. Due to a mild winter the quality and quantity of ice was insufficient to last through the summer.

The following spring (1969) he installed electric refrigerators in all the cottages that were owned and rented by the hotel. Nature's own ice for refrigeration at Harbour View became a thing of the past.

Mostly we used the ice for ginger ale and ginger beer, but the grown-ups put it in other beverages as well. Up until 1933 the United States went through a ridiculous and highly unnatural phase called Prohibition. Because the sale, manufacture and consumption of beverage alcohol was declared illegal by the U.S. Constitution, many people who might not have considered doing so otherwise, began to drink.

As the moonshine product was vile stuff, Canada prospered greatly by providing and transporting liquor of decent quality across the border by land and by sea. The majority of Maritime seafaring men were then engaged in rum-running for at least several trips, and rum-running stories were high on their list of favorite topics for decades afterwards.

Canadian tourism also benefited from Prohibition because Americans could buy and consume decent liquor as long as it wasn't done in a public place. (Some consider "decent liquor" a shameful oxymoron, but they must not have tasted moonshine.)

Cocktail parties were very popular and frequent events at Harbor View during Prohibition, and so were card parties. My parents decided to have a card party once, but then they found no poker chips were available. So for days we all sat around cutting out uniform discs from sheets of red, blue and white cardboard.

Entering the United States from Canada during Prohibition was a tedious and unpleasant affair. All luggage was opened and all people were suspected of being criminals by U. S. Customs inspectors. Entering Canada then was a breeze—cordial greetings by border personnel and never a search or a shred of suspicion at all. The situation is now reversed—and to what end? Official paranoia should be outlawed all along our peaceful common border.

No cottage owner bothered to raise vegetables; there was no need because we ate at the hotel. Elsewhere, both vegetable gardens and flower gardens were seen all along every road. Nova Scotians were more self-sufficient (and poorer) than now, and patronized stores only for what they could not or did not produce themselves. This was true of rural people all over North America at that time, especially during the Great Depression.

Of course, there were no supermarkets; these were not even heard of until after World War II. The general store prevailed and there were many of them. Weir's store in Smith's Cove was a typical general store that sold everything from toothpaste and canned peas to rubber boots, rope and kerosene lamps.

Flower gardens were abundant and lush at that time. That was probably influenced by two facts: times were hard, particularly in Nova Scotia, and labor was cheap; also there were many horses and oxen and consequently an abundance of manure was at hand. Manure and labor are the two chief ingredients of a good flower garden.

Mark Longworth was Nanny's gardener. He was a great, burly bull of a man with formidable, bushy, straw-colored eyebrows and thick, blond wool on his chest and arms to match his eyebrows. He always had an unlit pipe in his mouth and a greasy straw hat on his half-bald head. He was apparently born without a neck.

He scowled at everybody and I was sure he was born that way, too. He growled at children and we were terrified of him. When he spoke, which was rarely, I could not understand him. Indeed his Yorkshire accent was a foreign language and he never modified it.

He had come out to Canada after World War I to marry Miss Stella Austin, a refined young lady he had known only by mail. Miss Austin had put her name and address in the toe of a pair of socks she had knitted for the soldiers in World War I and he had replied.

The Longworths had a large but mentally defective son, of whom all the children in the village were afraid. He would hide in the lilac hedge by the entrance to Harbor View Road and suddenly emerge.

No doubt Mr. Longworth had reason to have a sour disposition, and Mrs. Longworth even more so. But Mrs. Longworth took everything that life dealt her with a cheerful nature and found time to be the mainstay of the Smith's Cove Tennis Club, with its court on the east corner across from the United (Methodist) Church. Teddy Roosevelt played on that now overgrown court. (Roosevelt would not allow himself to be photographed sweating. Therefore he never was photographed playing tennis, a game that he loved, or in tennis garb. He could play to his heart's content in Smith's Cove without the clicking of shutters—and sweat all he pleased.)

Mr. Longworth was an outstanding gardener and soon had Nanny's new cottage surrounded by snap dragons, hollyhocks, delphiniums and tiger lilies, and had pillar roses blooming on trellises on both the front and back. "Longworth," as the grown-ups called him, also kept the lawn mowed and rolled so well that we could have fairly reliable games of croquet on it.

Bob Milbank told me about Mr. Longworth's unusual way of billing for his work:

> In a bill he sent my father he itemized the expense as follows:
>
> Horse_____hours @_____/hour = $_____
>
> Self _____hours @_____/hour = $_____
>
> Total $
>
> While the horse worked fewer hours than Longworth, we were surprised that the hourly rate for the horse was greater than the rate for Self.

Summer was a wonderful time, punctuated by wonderful events. One of these, at least for us children, was haying.

There were a number of hay meadows on the Harbor View property then. The mowing machine, a pair of wheels with a seat between them and a sickle bar on one side, was pulled back and forth by a single horse (Belgian, I believe). The following day the same horse would pull the hay rake and the operator would line the hay up in long windrows so that the air could flow through it and thus accelerate drying and curing. The next day men and boys would be out there with rakes and forks working the windrows into piles and then pitching the piles up onto the hay wagon pulled by the same horse.

We little kids would help by distributing the hay in the wagon so as to build the largest possible load and to keep it from falling off. We also had to keep out ohe way of the sharp, three-pronged hay forks and each new forkful of hay. Actually we were more tolerated than useful, but it was great fun for us. It seemed that the hottest weather was reserved for haying.

The hotel grew all its own fresh vegetables, but these were never in season when we arrived in July. Consequently there were only canned vegetables until the garden began to produce. Everyone celebrated when these fresh things came into the dining room and one by one the canned foods were dropped for that year.

Few fresh fruits and vegetables were shipped any distance then, and packaged frozen food was not yet invented. All the milk was local and often came to the table with flecks of yellow cream floating on it. Sometimes it had an unusual flavor, depending upon what the cow had been eating.

There was no such thing as margarine, but there was plenty of real butter. There was no homogenized, 1% or 2% milk. Rich, yellow cream separated from the milk automatically and floated on the top if the milk stood a while.

The village of Smith's Cove boasted two important commercial establishments then: Weir's store and Payson's garage. Mail was distributed from the old post office by a man in a dusty black buggy with "H M MAIL" lettered crudely on the back in dusty white paint.

Miss Louise Jaggar played the organ at the birch chapel every Sunday. She walked through the dark woods from Kelpie, her house on the point overlooking Digby and the Joggin.

No sun could penetrate into this moss-covered trail. Waxy white Indian pipes and a multitude of colorful toadstools and mushrooms grew among the moss and rotting stumps and tree trunks. Half way through this magic forest a wooden gate barred the way and bore an ominous sign, "BULL GATE – KEEP CLOSED."

It took me several years to muster enough courage to go beyond that gate. It actually took Miss Jaggar's smile and invitation to convince me that I would not be gored and that her house was worth seeing.

She was a charming carry-over from former years in that she dressed in the style of the 1890s. She always wore a full-length white dress with a high lace collar, which was kept up by whalebone stays, and full-length sleeves with puffy shoulders. I never saw her without a broad-brimmed white hat and pince-nez glasses loosely attached to her neck with a black ribbon. Outdoors in fair weather she carried a white, long-handled parasol with frilly edges. She had a thin shadow of a black moustache, and was very kind.

Kelpie was unique in every way. The main room was two storeys high (that was before cathedral ceilings became popular) and was built especially to accomodate a large, stained-glass church window that was given to her father, Bishop Jaggar, when he retired from his post in the Diocese of Boston. The window was impressive, but it blocked what could have been a superb view of Digby Gut.

One long wall was lined with books, clear to the ceiling, with a ladder and balcony to make them all accessible.

All Jaggar family members were artists and they had painted a series of small wooden panels to resemble Delft tiles. Each blue-and-white tile showed a different scene of special significance to the family and they were all mounted around the opening of the fireplace in the dining room.

That dining room had two other features that made it legendary. The English ivy on the south side of the house had grown in around the dining room window sash and had entwined itself around the antlers of a deer's head mounted on the wall. At the other end of the room was a large oil painting of a lion (life-size) painted, I believe, by Bishop Jaggar. The painting was actually the door to a secret passage that led into the cellar.

Kelpie had an enormous barn right on the point of land blocking the view to the west. The road to Kelpie entered between two stone posts (still there) at the end of what most people called Lover's Lane, much of which is now within the campgrounds.

Kelpie and the barn no longer stand, having burned to the ground right after World War II.

After the fire the Jaggar family sold the land to Walter Flett, the then-new proprietor of Harbour View. One winter storm blew down many spruce trees on this land and Flett gave permission to someone who had inquired about the windfalls to "take whatever you want."

When Walter Flett returned from Halifax in the spring he was chagrined to see the entire Jaggar property had been logged and that his "take whatever you want" had been taken too literally and stretched beyond merely the fallen spruce that he had intended.

When Flett sold Harbour View to David and Sylvia Irvine, he sold the Jaggar land to Russell Fries, who later built there, but farther to the north than Kelpie and farther away from the campground.

A large wooded area along the Fries driveway was found to be infested with spruce bark beetle. Bear River Woodlands (Harold Clapp) clear-cut the area and planted red pines. Those trees are now over 18 feet tall.

One relic remains of Miss Louise Jaggar. My father bought an oil painting from her for five dollars in the early thirties. It is of a woods road in early October. Miss Jaggar painted it on unprimed canvas, a practice that was not uncommon at the time. She never signed the painting, but I attest that she painted it.

Nanny and Mrs. Richardson, wife of the archbishop of Fredericton, were good friends. The Richardson's grand-daughter, Dorothea Claridge, and I used to play together. I was awed by the fact that she could speak French—had to because she lived on the Gaspé.

Mrs. Richardson gave me my first cup of tea on her verandah—cambric tea with lots of milk and sugar. The only thing weaker would have been "pearl tea," which contains no tea at all, only hot water, milk and sugar.

Bishop Richardson had a small study built for him so as to be away from the distractions of his family: Bert and Helen Claridge of Matane, PQ and their two children, Dorothea and John; his other daughters Phyllis, Edith and Mary; Mrs. Richardson and numerous guests. On the wall of the bishop's study was a sign that read, 'Peace, perfect peace, with loved ones far away.'

In this much-savored solitude he composed many inspiring sermons and people came from some distance to hear him preach. Bob Milbank confessed to me that he was attracted to both the

Richardsons' raspberry patch and to Mary, who was his age.

The eleven o'clock service at the chapel was always well-attended, usually packed. Mr. Cossitt, its builder and its senior warden, rang the bell. For fifty years he rang it, and after he died, Dr. Shenstone took over.

Rosie Paul, in full Mi'kmaq regalia, would kneel on the porch with palms pressed together from before the final bell until after the benediction. I doubt that she understood enough English to derive full meaning from what was said or sung there, but she paid her respects to the Great Spirit in her own pious way and led an honorable life.

Rosie spent her summers in a birch bark and tar paper wigwam in the lee of the point, and just south of where David and Sylvia Irvine's boathouse now stands. Fifty feet away was a spring of clear water surrounded by ferns and touch-me-nots. There, seated on the ground inside or in front of that humble abode, Rosie wove baskets. She made them of maple and ash splints, birch bark, sweet grass and porcupine quills. Indian men would come with supplies for her and would pound and split the ash for her.

She dyed many of the maple splints so that her finished products were delightful to look at. The ash she never dyed. That was for making sturdy items like laundry baskets and pack baskets to carry into the woods.

Often Fannie Pictou would be with Rosie. Fanny knew no English and smoked a pipe. She was morose, but she wove beautiful baskets the same as Rosie did.

There was a boy my age with them sometimes. He and I would run through the woods together and help Rosie pick sweet grass from the marsh at the edge of the meadow.

Sweet grass grows only in a narrow band between a salt marsh and higher ground. It is an inconspicuous grass with a heavenly fragrance that lingers for years. It is light green and its blades are flat, but they curl up longitudinally as they dry. When first picked, sweetgrass is odorless. The fragrance develops as the grass cures.

All of Rosie's maple splint baskets and all those she made of birch bark were trimmed along the lip with dried sweet grass. Its aroma brings life and romance into any room where it is.

Trimming baskets is the only use for sweet grass that most white men understand. But to Indians it has a greater significance and use. To them it is holy.

When three thin bundles are braided together and dried they are a reminder of the trinity of life (body, mind and spirit) that is in all creatures and of the relatedness of all life. A smudge is made with the braid and the smoke is waved in the four directions to acknowledge the universality of life and the supremacy of the Great Spirit. Smoke is wafted at a person as a blessing and as a reminder that he is one with all creation. Then the person reverently scoops the smoke with his hands over his head and face as a cleansing and sanctifying ritual.

One summer just before World War II, we returned to Smith's Cove and found no Indians and no Indian camp. Local white men had burned down the camp in the winter and made the Indians aware that they were no longer welcome at Harbor View.

Technically, according to the law of the white man, the Indians had been squatting on land they did not own. It didn't matter that their ancestors had camped in that very spot from the beginning— the first settlers after the ice age—certainly long before the French and English began squabbling and took their lands.

From this camp, Indian men ventured out onto the Basin in fragile birch bark canoes to harpoon porpoises and to fish. Until the twenties their men guided and took parties of whites into the woods for recreational hunting and fishing.

Indians didn't know how to own land and had no titles, no deeds, no legal documents. White men taught them about these things and stole from them with instruments of paper and the niceties of European civilization, under the banner and blessing of Christianity.

There was a fish weir made of brush on the south end of the Bear Island bar. Bob Milbank tells the following about the weir:

> I was intrigued to see oxen drawing a small wagon there at low tide. One day I walked out there and discovered the driver was shoveling fish into the wagon. Low tide didn't last. Long, so I had to move fast to get back—no time to linger and ask questions.

With the harvest of herring from this weir, a smoke house on the shore near Bear River station was kept busy producing kippers, most of which were exported.

When we occupied Nanny's new cottage, *Sunnymeade*, she and

my mother had a wonderful time buying things for it. Hooked rugs were high on their shopping list. There was an abundance of them available; it seemed that nearly every woman in the area produced them and hung them by the roadside for sale.

Some were works of art and demonstrated high degrees of imagination and original design. Most were beautiful examples of burlap and rags converted into cheerful traditional patterns—truly silk purses made of sow's ears. All of them were tedious to make. I know; I tried.

Along with our new cottage came Jenny Rice. Jenny came every morning to make the beds and clean. She had led a hard life, having been beaten repeatedly by her stepfather. Her nose, broken and never set, lay to one side of her face to vouch for his attentions.

There were a number of local Smith's Cove girls who walked in every morning to make beds, clean and get the coal burning in the pot stoves that heated water in every cabin. Of these "cabin girls" there were the cheery and hard-working Winchester sisters: Hilda, Sue, Maude, Ada May and Dorothy. Ada May was Bob Milbank's first Nova Scotian nursemaid.

Waitresses were mostly college girls who received room and board, small pay and tips. Mary Lou (Mrs. Kelsey) Raymond came first to Smith's Cove as a waitress in 1951.

When I was seven my brother Robert was born. Bob got off to a bad start, having been severely ill with pneumonia soon after he was born. I remember being taken into his sick room for one last look at his pale, still form before he died.

But he did not die.

When he came to Smith's Cove, Lillian Adams was engaged to take care of him. She stayed with us full-time and practically became part of the family. She had been a teacher and had taught in one of the one-room schoolhouses that dotted the roadsides—a time when all children walked to school.

Lillian fitted in so well, and was so much appreciated by us all, that for several years she went back and forth to New Jersey and spent the winters with us.

At some point I learned to dive before I learned to swim. The little slip at the beach was a perfect place to play this game. One day when I was in the care of a Mrs. Dexter, someone I have never seen before and have never seen since, I dove farther and farther out on the slip. Finally I dove into water that was over my head and

I could not stand up.

I was suddenly in severe trouble, and would have drowned if it were not for a Mr. Chaney, who was waiting on the beach to be picked up by a boat. He yanked me out while Mrs. Dexter, who was terrified of the water, stood by miserably wringing her hands.

Except for his shoes, Mr. Chaney's fine yachting clothes were drenched. The last I saw of him he was hanging his clothes in the rigging to dry as he sailed away around the point.

I witnessed another interesting event at the beach one day. The tide was high about two o'clock one sunny Sunday and there was a whole crowd of people gathered at the water's edge at the foot of the road. A man, fully dressed, stood in the cold water and, one by one, immersed people who waded out to him. He gravely pushed them over backwards until they were completely submerged. They held their noses and remained stiff. They appeared to be dressed in something like white sheets.

The people on the beach had a fine time keeping dry and singing hymns.

Although my mother drove well and enjoyed it (she had driven an ambulance during World War I), Nanny had to have a chauffeur. So she engaged Lloyd Adams for the job. He was Lillian's brother and a special hero of mine. Later on, for a short time, Garnet Adams drove for her.

Nanny's big black Buick was kept in the garage, a building between the barn and the road consisting of many stalls with doors and connected in a single row. Part of this building still stands, but it is slowly succumbing to rot and is probably held up only by all the stuff stored in it.

Once a week we would drive up after supper to Mrs. Potter's house. Mrs. Potter did our laundry, and we would exchange the clean batch with her for the dirty things. In thinking back now, I suspect that the reason the clean laundry always smelled strongly of soap was that Mrs. Potter had to draw all the water by windlass from the well and used it sparingly for rinsing.

Laundry was done in a round, galvanized tub with a washboard standing in it. A cake of brown laundry soap and plenty of scrubbing by hand were all that was needed, together with hot water.

We kept a washboard under the kitchen sink in our cottage in case something could not wait for Mrs. Potter. It is still there, but we haven't used it in many years.

Mrs. Potter always looked tired and was usually cranking the cream separator when we arrived. As I liked to turn cranks, I usually was allowed to work the cream separator and to hoist up a pailful of water for her.

More important for me was that Mr. William Potter had oxen and cows, and that one side of his barn roof sloped down to within three feet of the ground. It was just right to climb on – right up to its high ridgepole.

The view from Mr. Potter's barn roof was good because the north slope of Hardscrabble Hill was all cleared then and was devoted entirely to farming. When you came in through Digby Gut, the most striking feature of the Annapolis Basin was this clean hillside with its neatly outlined fields.

Now Otis Robbins' fields are the only open ones left, but they may not be for long. He has given up farming and sold his animals. He is badly crippled and the forest is reclaiming his fields.

There were no paved roads before the late thirties, and every trip by car had to be made with extra time allowed for flat tires. Dust was everywhere along the road. When another car approached, all windows were cranked up until that car's dust had dispersed. Of course there was no such thing as air conditioning in houses, stores, theaters, and especially in cars.

Few of the children alongside the road wore shoes; all men and most boys wore either patched overalls or suspenders. The children waved vigorously and smiled at every passing car.

When work began in preparation for paving the road up from Yarmouth (I forget the year) we counted 125 yoke of oxen working on the road between Yarmouth and Smith's Cove. This work must have been a welcome boon to everyone along the way who owned oxen.

A cataclysmic event took place September 9, 1938. That was when the hotel burned down.

The fire was discovered at 12:45 by Mr. Theodore Nesbitt as he was walking down to eat. Twenty guests were already eating at the time.

The fire started just under the roof from the leaky chimney that served the living room fireplace.

The waitresses who lived on the third floor lost everything they had. Most of the contents of the second and first floors (furniture, records and kitchen equipment) were saved.

The loss of the hotel was figured to be $18,000, only part of which was covered by insurance. Fortunately there was no loss of life and there were no injuries.

Kelsey Raymond's favorite recollection of the fire was that of eating his fill of blueberry pie as it was brought out of the kitchen and of watching china wash basins, mirrors and pitchers being thrown out the second storey windows. (At the same time mattresses and pillows were carefully carried downstairs.)

My Uncle Dave, an artist who was then living in Bear River and who happened to be at the Bear River fire hall when the alarm came in, rode over on the fire engine and watched the uncontrollable fire consume the entire large frame structure except for the back stairs to the dining room. The firemen could only spray water on the first cottage behind the hotel (#14, now the Wetmores'). Many summer people were there as it was dinnertime. In the excitement everybody pitched in and did whatever was at hand.

Barbara Milbank (now Mrs. Lawrence VanDoren of South Orange, NJ) wrote:

> As for the hotel fire, I remember that event vividly. We were on our way down to lunch before driving to Yarmouth to sail back to New York. As we were walking down we noticed smoke coming from the upper portion of the Hotel.
>
> By the time we reached the building it was a full-blown fire. We went into the dining room and gathered up tablecloths right off the tables with the cutlery and dishes inside and carried them to the tennis court.
>
> Some people were so panicky they were heaving the porch chairs off the porch and my mother was telling them to carry them so they would not break.
>
> Fire engines came from Bear River as well as Digby, but that took time.
>
> We had to leave to catch the boat, but as we drove off the flames were high and the wind was blowing toward the cabins. The fire fighters were hosing down the roofs of the closest cabins.

The casino roof caught fire from the sparks, but the firemen managed to limit this damage. This did not prevent the regular dance schedule from being adhered to. As asphalt shingles had not yet been adopted in Smith's Cove, all roofs then were covered with wood shingles, the best kind of kindling available.

Since the hotel fire, wooden shingles on all Harbour View roofs have been replaced by fire-retardant asphalt ones (and recently, on #10, a bright red steel roof, guaranteed for fifty years).

When wooden roofing shingles were used, leaks were common. To stop a leak, the method most often used was to cut a flattened tin can into a suitable rectangular size and force it under the shingles where the leak originated. Such pieces of tin lasted fairly well, as the tin coating on cans was far thicker than is used today.

I was privileged to have a great deal of freedom to roam and explore. I delighted in riding on wagons and marveling at the power and patience of the horses and oxen that pulled them.

One day I attached myself to John Sibley, who was fetching a load of gravel from the beach. He stood on the narrow board on the very front of the wagon and called out to his oxen (I believe they were named Allen and Bright) and tickled them with his whip. As he was my current role model, I had to stand on that board beside him.

The wagon lurched over a stone and I fell in front of the right front wheel. John jumped down and dashed in front of the oxen, who, with their unthinking brute strength, were devoting themselves wholeheartedly to hauling those tons up the hill. He was able to stop the animals just as the steel-rimmed wheel was an inch or two from my head. I must have been dazed by the fall for I did not move.

Leaving the wagon where it was, he carried me in his arms across the field to Sunnymeade.

John was a war veteran who had served in France, as my father had. In gratitude for saving my life, my father gave him twenty dollars. The following Sunday John showed up at our cottage wearing a big smile and the handsome new suit he had bought with the money.

Firewood was stacked in four-foot lengths and cut into usable lengths by a cordwood saw. This saw was generally powered by a make-and-break one-cylinder engine, but as time went on the practice changed to the use of a belt powered from the jacked-up rear wheel of an old car or truck. There was a stop that was set to whatever length wood was wanted. 24-inch wood was called "one-cut" wood, 16-inch wood was "two-cut" wood and 12-inch wood was called "three-cut" or "stove" wood.

Saturday nights were when local people flocked to Digby. People piled into trucks that hauled pulpwood during the week, but for Saturday nights and Sunday outings were fitted with wooden benches.

The movies were the greatest attraction, but often the trip to town was made just to see other people and maybe to buy something. Nothing happened there on Sundays except church, and the town was dead.

Bear River had its annual spree in the form of its Cherry Carnival. There were all kinds of games and such guide contests as canoe tilting, log rolling, canoe racing, climbing the greased pole and speed chopping with a double-bladed axe. The Indian community turned out in traditional garb and sold all sorts of things that they had made.

To see Bear River today one would not believe it possible for the town to have been packed with people, activity and excitement. Trucks and cars carried people to the Cherry Carnival from as far as Weymouth and Bridgetown.

Bear River's cherry trees were famous for their sweet, succulent dark cherries, many crates of which were exported.

The Cherry Carnival raised money for charity, and most Harbor View people participated in some way. One year a Harbor View lady played Fortune Teller and Harold Milbank was the man at the door to the small tent. He would casually engage the "Next Customer" in conversation, learn something about the person and share it with the Fortune teller when he entered the tent to see if she was ready for the "Next Customer."

Bear River has continued the economic decline that began with the pulp mill incident. A blight struck the cherry trees after World War II and most of them were cut down. Each year now there is a "Cherry Carnival," but it is a sparsely-attended, pale ghost of the events held in more boisterous and prosperous days. Cherries for the event are imported.

During the Vietnam War a number of draft evaders and hippies from the United States sought refuge in Bear River. They found a shriveled population, largely elderly, and cheap housing, some vacant and begging to be occupied.

The new arrivals created an economic revival in Bear River which has not been sustained by the local population. The locals resented the energy and success of these young Americans.

Well after their arrival Bear River became inundated with illegal drugs and remains so still. Since then most of the former draft evaders and hippies have left and the picturesque village has slipped back to its old stagnation, and worse, this time having earned the reputation of being a center for drugs and users of drugs, both sellers and users being native locals.

But there is hope. Two who arrived during the Vietnam era have bought the old Oakdene School and have converted it into a center for community activities, including a satellite of the local Community College. Nothing in life or history is static.

Bear River's small industries dropped off one by one: the blacksmith shop across from the fire hall, the barrel stave mill at the head of the tide on the point between the East and West branches of the river, even the candle factory (a recent enterprise dating from the Vietnam War days) disappeared and were not replaced with anything. After two armed robberies, the Royal Bank closed its Bear River branch in 1993 and sent its customers to Digby.

Aside from a few shops and two gas stations, there is little to entice a visitor except the lingering charm of the unusual terrain and the charming architecture. It is, however, a Mecca for photographers and painters, and for visitors to its outstanding arts and crafts store, "Flight of Fancy."

Before World War II it was unthinkable for any Harbor View guest or summer person to do any manual work. The "Do-It-Yourself" era had not yet arrived. Gentlemen could get as dirty as they wanted if they dug clams (we used these for clam-bakes and for bait when we handlined in the cove; it took only a few minutes to find a dozen or so big ones), or to putter around the flower garden, provided a man was hired to do the digging and the heavy sweating. In fact, the Victorian view of sweat still prevailed: "Horses sweat; gentlemen perspire; ladies glow."

Trains, ships and industry

The tracks of the Dominion Atlantic Railway (DAR) crossed Harbour View Road to the south of the Annex. Just to the northeast of the road was the tiny Imbertville station. Trains stopped there to deliver passengers and their baggage, and to pick up passengers when the passenger moved the red flag from inside the station out to the hole in the cornerpost of the building.

Mail was also picked up and delivered there. The arriving mail bag was just kicked out the mail car door onto the cinders alongside. The outgoing mail was hung in an ingenious contraption. The bag's top and bottom were held by clips on the ends of two arms that protruded from a vertical post. The mailman in the mail car extended a steel rod with a gentle hook in its end so that as the rod struck the center of the mail bag it would swing downward and sweep the bag unfailingly into the open door. The rod was a permanent fixture in the doorway and pivoted so as to be always ready to grab. The train did not need to stop to pick up the mail, merely slow down.

The locomotives were massive things fueled by coal and the strong arms and back of the fireman, and driven by steam and the engineer's skill. These puffing mammoths were painted maroon, black and gold and were always carefully oiled and polished.

They had names that seemed like magic at the time. There was Poutrincourt, de Monts, Biencourt and other names of the early French explorers.

The engineer never failed to give us a big smile and a wave. He always wore the traditional finely-striped engineer's cap, striped overalls and a red bandana.

We heard his magic whistle a long time before the train arrived at Imbertville station. Long, long, short, long—"Q" in Morse code, short for Queen, in honor of Queen Victoria. Although George the Fifth was on the throne, the old queen still reigned the rails.

This signal sounded long and loud before the train reached each of the great many grade crossings. All the whistling not withstanding, Kelsey Raymond's car was hit on two occasions in the 1980s as he drove up his driveway.

There were three railway stations in Smith's Cove then: Smith's Cove (where the tracks crossed the Mountain Gap Inn driveway), Imbertville (at Harbor View) and Bear River (not at Bear River at all, but directly south of the Bear Island sand bar.)

The Smith's Cove station was eliminated after World War II. The station building was hauled down the road and used for many years as part of the Bon-e-Lass Restaurant, which still stands, although unused for several years.

Of the three, only the Bear River station was ever manned. The station master took care of all passenger needs and handled all the baggage and freight. He also operated the telegraph, which was powered by a roomful of wet batteries: large, rectangular, green glass jars with electrodes and wires, and with a blue-green liquid in them. That station had a siding, and the station master operated the switches for it.

The station was torn down in the early 1970s.

The railway bridge over the Bear River and the Victoria Bridge beside it were cranked open by hand to allow ships to pass through. Fletcher Adams, who lived in the big white house at this end of the Victoria Bridge, operated the railway bridge single-handedly by walking round and round pushing the removable capstan bar in the middle of the swinging span. He had twelve children, including Lloyd, Lillian and Garnet, who were very important to our family.

There was a wharf attached to the middle of the Victoria Bridge on both upstream and downstream sides. Waterborne freight was loaded and unloaded there for the convenience of Smith's Cove and Deep Brook. Occasionally a schooner would tie up there and load with pulp wood. Even with the light traffic of those days, this operation would cause lengthy delays for cars and trucks crossing the bridge. There was often congestion on the bridge anyhow, due to its being only one lane wide and rather long.

Around the end of World War II the old one-lane bridge was fitted with a traffic light. This prevented many debates about whether the eastbound or westbound traffic should cross first and somebody having to back up.

A new bridge was built beside it in 1972 and the old relic was torn down the following year. The new bridge is of a radical new design and, as shipping in and out of Bear River had completely died, it lacks the ability to open for water traffic. The new bridge was built of pre-cast and pre-stressed hollow segments that were strung together on wire cables, much the same as a string of beads, and laid across a series of concrete piers.

The success of this bridge caused it to be copied and built in larger scale versions elsewhere, including the Interstate Route 95 crossing of the Connecticut River in 1993.

The appearance of the Bear River packet was a frequent occurrence. It was a small steamer named the *SS Elizabeth Cann*. It ran between Saint John, Digby, Bear River, Annapolis and sometimes up the river as far as Bridgetown. Occasionally the larger *SS Keith Cann* made the run in her place. The packet served up until 1945.

There was other ocean-going traffic, too. Every summer several gypsum boats would put in to the wharf at the gypsum "plant" on the point across from us in Deep Brook and load gypsum from the big, white, sheet-metal storage shed. Gypsum was shipped there by train from quarries in the Windsor area because of inadequate port facilities in Windsor, especially in winter.

When the storage shed was erected it was the largest building (in area) in the world. It took twenty-six freighters to empty the shed when operations ceased. The building was torn down and sold for scrap in the early 1970s.

There were schooners, too, that passed slowly in front of us on their way to load lumber at Bear River. There were very few of these, for the era in which they were economically profitable to operate had already passed.

A large brick mill building stood downstream from the railway bridge on the Deep Brook side of the Bear River. It was referred to as either the "pulp mill" or "Clark's mill." It contained giant boilers and other steel vessels and machinery, but was otherwise empty, silent and open to the curious wanderer.

The mill was a local disaster. It had been promoted to utilize a new process for producing wood pulp by using salt water, which had never been possible before. Without testing the process in a pilot plant, funds were raised and the mill was built. The process did not work.

To salvage the venture, a wooden stave pipeline was run in from a small lake nearby to bring fresh water. In no time the lake was sucked dry and the mill closed forever—a total loss.

Most of the people in the Bear River area who had any money or who owned wood lots invested everything they could scrape together, including the proceeds from the sale of their land. Every penny of it was lost and bitterness and economic decline set in and changed the face and the future of Bear River.

For decades sections of the wooden pipe were used for culverts, drains, watering troughs and many other domestic uses, particularly to improve numerous roadside springs by sinking a vertical two-foot section into seepages at the foot of gravel banks. The first worthwhile use to which the mill building was put was to manufacture travel trailers in the late 1960s. Later it was used as headquarters for Beaver Marine while they built the Bear River bridge and the new ferry wharf in the Gut at Rattling Beach. In 1993 a feeble start was made to tear the building down, but it remains a worse eyesore than ever and a bitter reminder to old-timers.

Pennies in those days were valuable. One penny would buy a good-sized piece of candy. Five of them would buy a large candy bar or an ice cream cone or one hot dog. A penny would also make a wonderful souvenir if, after much deliberation, it was placed on the railway track and squashed out long and thin by the weight of a massive steam locomotive. These were big souvenirs because the large one cent pieces were then in use.

The main road between Yarmouth and Halifax ran through the village and right past the entrance to Harbour View Road. It wasn't until 1972 that the new Route 101 was built and most of the traffic rerouted high above the village.

This spelled the demise of the garage that had so long served the area. It was Payson's Garage before World War II. Owners after Ned Payson were, successively, Ted Miller, Raymond Moore, Frank Miller ('60s), Henry Sarty (late '60s and early '70s), two others for a short time, then Karl and Jan Abbott. Eventually it was torn down in 1992.

Digby has its own airport out on the "Ridge." At first its only building was a retired school bus. Now it has a satisfactory terminal building, but no scheduled service. Digby's airport has the distinction of having fewer fogbound days than the one at Yarmouth, but this fact has been insufficient to entice Air Canada to make scheduled stops there. For a brief time (less than a year)

Digby was serviced by Air Bras d'Or, a tiny airline that ran commuter-size planes between Bangor, Saint John, Digby, Halifax and Sydney. Air Bras d'Or is now defunct.

In fact, the importance of western Nova Scotia has diminished in the eyes of Air Canada, the only airline ever to serve the area, to the point of flying only one two-engine, propeller-driven plane a day from Boston to Yarmouth. That is an hour and a quarter versus the fifty-five minute flight previously made by each of their several jet airplane flights each day. Sadly, even that limited service was discontinued in 1997.

Both Yarmouth and Digby airports are available for use, but the only scheduled flights are to Halifax and Saint John, New Brunswick.

A ray of economic hope shines on our area in 1997. This bit of optimism comes from a project of a Manitoba Mennonite company. They intend to set up a tire recycling operation in the Cornwallis compound. They will employ seventy-five people. That leaves many acres and many fine buildings vacant and unused.

For several years all imaginable rumors have circulated about how the former naval training station will be utilized. Perhaps it remains for something as positive as Hong Kong money, imagination and business acumen to bring out the full economic potential of the complex. A new perspective is needed.

Beach, boats and Bear Island

People used the beach at Harbour View more in former days. We actually swam there. A little slip ran down the beach and served as a boat landing and as a convenient place to swim from during the top four or five hours of each tide. Each winter heavy nor'east storms would severely damage it; each spring it was repaired or rebuilt.

The best times to swim were when the tide was high around three o'clock on a clear, hot day. The sun's heat would warm the beach gravel and the gravel would temper the water coming in over it.

There was a bathhouse, no more than a row of little connected closets, in which one could change into a bathing suit.

The first swimming "pool" was built in the early twenties. "Pool" is too elegant a name for it, as it was simply a rectangular, unlined pit excavated in the marsh just above the beach. The stiff marsh soil and the vegetation kept the sides fairly stable and vertical. A ditch was dug to a little below the high tide line so that water could flow in at high tide, but the ditch was not deep enough to allow much to flow out as the tide ebbed. Thus the pool water remained considerably warmer than that in the Basin and was topped off and freshened twice daily by the tide. The bathhouses were placed beside the pool and the pool was equipped with a diving board.

Unfortunately it was difficult to maintain the pool and it soon became unpleasant, except for the thousands of minnows that thrived there, because of algae and the pool's gradual filling with mud. Sheet erosion added solid fill from the hay meadow above it and winter storms washed in gravel and sand. No trace of the pool remains now and the marsh is quite dry most of the time.

In 1947, after World War II, Walter Flett built a proper concrete pool below the tennis court. It stands there today[4]. At first, how-

---

4   The pool was filled in in 2016-17. Its remains are under the broad lawn north of the new pool.

ever, it was filled with salt water pumped up from the beach during several successive high tides. As the intake was covered with water for only the top four hours of the tide, it took two days (four tides equaling 16 hours of pumping) to fill the pool. After filling, the pool was so cold its only practical use was for a quick dip.

After a few days of summer sun warmed the water, it became quite pleasant until the water became foul and had to be drained, and the empty pool scrubbed out. There was no filtration or recirculation system.

To accommodate salt water, the pump was all brass and the piping asbestos cement. The motor, however, was an ancient Briggs and Stratton for which parts were no longer available. In 1967 it died and was scrapped, and the use of salt water was discontinued.

A filtration system was installed and the pool was filled with fresh water from the same prodigious well that still serves the rest of the colony. This way it now takes two weeks to fill the pool, but the water is replenished, recirculated and filtered all summer and remains pristine. Water passing through the filter then runs through a coil of black plastic pipe on the pump house roof. This warms the water on sunny days and chills it every night and on cloudy days.

We children were the only ones to walk on the gravel with bare feet. Others either wore old sneakers, preferably with holes in the toes to let them drain, or special bathing slippers. Much to my surprise these things are now back on the market (trademarked "Aqua-Sox") and are the "in" thing for and young old alike.

The beach gravel was finer then and had much sand in it. After ownership of Harbour View fell into the hands of Walter Flett of Halifax, enormous quantities of this fine beach gravel were mined and hauled away, leaving an unpleasant beach of egg- and walnut-size stones. Since then the beach gradually has returned to its previous degree of fineness, the sandy material having been washed in from eroding banks farther out on the point.

Removing beach gravel or stones below the mean high tide line is now forbidden under provincial law. Removing it from above the high tide line is tantamount to stealing it from the owners of that land.

Favorite beach activities for children included skipping stones, picking up lucky stones with stripes around them and sailing toy boats.

A slip had been previously located just north of the present David Irvine cottage where the beach is steep, but during my years it was always at the foot of the road to the beach, the present Beachcomber Lane. It was better for swimming there, the gravel finer, the water warmer and it was less windy.

The slip was convenient for loading passengers and into boats. Several of these were moored out on the mud gear flats. All had open cockpits, whether sail or power boats.

There were frequent picnics and expeditions, particularly to Bear Island. The Rices' house on Bear Island stood largely in ruins when I can first remember it. The main remaining feature of it was the staircase that used to lead up to the second floor. We could climb the stairs and survey the wreckage from the top. The stairs must have been well built to have outlasted the rest of the structure.

The ice house, however, stood intact well into the thirties, and the stone ballast remains of the sturdy island slip can still be seen.

Bear Island has changed. The bar that connects it to the mainland was only exposed at spring low tides in the thirties. On rare occasions then a horse-drawn, two-wheeled cart would make the trip to the island, but I never found out for what reason. Storms and currents have swept material from the island toward the mouth of the Bear River and built up the bar so that it is now exposed at every low tide, even the neaps.

Two hundred years ago there was another, smaller island just to the east of Bear Island. All that remains of that today is a dangerous reef topped off by some unforgiving rocks. When the new highway bridge across the Bear River was built and it became impossible for ocean-going traffic to pass up the river, the buoy marking this reef was removed.

Bear Island was deeded to "the youth of Digby" by Dave Landers of Digby, who owned the island after the Rices. The island is administered by a committee consisting of the Mayor of Digby, the Chairman of the Digby School Board and the Chairman of the Board of Trade.

As part of the Navy's program, Sea Cadets stationed at Cornwallis used the island for training and recreation purposes. The island was heavily wooded, with a beautiful stand of white spruce. Navy trespassers thinned out the trees on the southeast end in the fifties, making the remaining trees susceptible to damage by the winter nor'east gales. Thus weakened, many trees were blown down.

As the Sea Cadets were using the Harbour View beach to access the island, David Irvine prevailed on the Base Commander to have the island removed from the Sea Cadet program.

Then the spruce bark beetle arrived on the island in the eighties and the rest of the mature spruce succumbed to it. An attempt was made by a local woods contractor to salvage the dead spruce for use as pulp wood. We have heard two reasons for the abandonment of that project: 1) because sand driven into the bark by winter storms ruined their chain saw chains, and 2) because they had too much trouble booming the logs to shore and removing them from the water. The latter reason is the more likely.

Cormorants found the dead trees at the north end of the island perfect to nest in. Their droppings, abundant and chemically powerful, have killed the vegetation below the trees and have created an area of desolation that is now moving steadily down the length of the island. When all those trees fall, the cormorants will leave, and the process of new growth on the heavily fertilized island will begin again.

Meanwhile erosion continues at a faster than usual pace and the day when the island becomes a peninsula approaches more quickly.

Bear Island has always been prime nesting ground for the great black-backed gull and the herring gull. One night's camping out at the south end of the island will convince anyone that there are plenty of protective parent gulls who are concerned about the safety of their young and who scream, wheel and dive repeatedly while we humans, even when in tents and trying to sleep, are too near their nests.

In 1938 a friend and I surveyed Bear Island with the crudest of implements: a compass and a piece of string 100 feet long. From a starting point we laid the string out straight along the high tide mark and recorded its compass bearing. We did this all around the island until we arrived back at the starting mark. Then we transferred this information to a sheet of paper by drawing one inch increments representing each hundred feet, and again using the compass to orient these segments. This method showed the island to be narrower than we had thought it to be. The spruce thicket had been so dense that it took a long struggle to cross the island, thus making it seem quite wide to us.

The lagoon at the south end of Bear Island changes from year to year. Some years it is steep-sided and deep enough to bring in a small boat during the top two hours of the tide. Then it is a good place to swim and even to dive from the gravel bank. The rush of the current in and out gives an added thrill to swimming there.

Small boats have been moored in Sulis Cove (the cove in front of Harbour View) for as long as Europeans have lived here. The most effective and cheapest mooring is a wooden stake, say 3"-4" in diameter and no more than 4' long. A hole is drilled through the upper end, and the lower end is roughly pointed with an axe. Then another log is used to drive the stake into the mud, leaving a few inches exposed. The suction is powerful enough to hold a schooner in a gale, and the salt water and lack of oxygen keep the stake sound for at least ten years. The portion completely below the mud is preserved indefinitely.

I always used a stake mooring, as did Allen Shenstone, and attest to its dependability. The end of the mooring line was secured to a four-foot log with a hole through each end. The mooring pennant was attached to the other end. This was the only form of mooring used before the 1960s.

My father had a small clinker-built boat with a skeg. It was too heavy to carry up and down the beach and was too delicate to drag over the stones and gravel. He used a modified trip-line system for mooring it that worked well and avoided the use of a tender. In using it, however, one always needed to plan ahead and consider at what height of tide the boat would be wanted next.

The system was simple:

1. Pay the anchor line into the bow of the boat beginning with its upper end.
2. Hang the anchor on the boat with only its bill touching the stem.
3. Attach a light line (even cod line would do) to the crown of the anchor (where the flukes meet the shank) and pay this line out onto the beach so that the part nearest the anchor is on top.
4. Push the boat out from the shore, stern first, using an oar if desired so as to keep feet dry.
5. When the boat reaches the spot where you want the anchor

to be, yank suddenly on the trip line and the anchor will fall.
6. Run the remainder of the trip line up the beach and drop a fair size rock on it or tie it to a rock.

There is no strain on the trip line until you pull in the anchor. The prevailing southwest wind helps move the boat out from the beach, but the system is hard to manage at high tide against a strong nor'east wind.

Normally we could position the boat at high tide so it would be accessible during the top four hours of the tide. When the tide is not fully high, the time of accessibility can be extended.

My father had this boat, the *Pelican*, built in Delaps Cove in 1929 or 1930 for $25 or $30. I sold her to Kelsey Raymond in 1976 for $50, a fair example of the loss of purchasing power of the dollar.

In 1980 I bought *TANSTAAFL* (There Ain't No Such Thing As A Free Lunch) from John Hinton and sold her to Chris Hopgood in 1987. Chris gave her to Robbie Bays in 1995. She had deteriorated so badly that she may have been reduced to kindling by now. She was a 17-foot, open-cockpit Cape Island weir boat with a long-shaft four horsepower outboard. She was a perfect rig for running around the Basin with grandchildren, handlining, picnicking on Bear Island and running up to Bear River for ice cream cones— safe, steady and seaworthy. She had the comfort and charm of wooden boats, but also the nuisance of maintenance that is insep-arable from wooden construction.

My favorite boat was the 21-foot, gaff-rigged sloop of a radical design that I bought in 1940 from Allen Shenstone for $25. She had a 6' oak bowsprit, a long overhanging boom and a 6' beam. Al-though Dr. Shenstone had never named her, her flat shape and her incredible speed caused me to name her *Flying Saucer*. She was then an elderly 40-year-old and needed work. Evan Dunn in Digby renailed her and fitted her with a new boom and mast, all for $15 and a case of Black Horse ale. She sailed fast and wet and had a strong weather helm. She often beat the new Lightning with which Dr. Shenstone replaced her.

Having sailed many years on the Basin and studied many differ-ent rigs and designs, Dr. Shenstone was convinced that the Light-ning was the perfect design for the Basin. They sit well on the mud, come easily and comfortably to the beach to load and unload, are fast, handle easily and respond sensitively. They are good in a race.

Hoping to establish them as the class that would replace the old sailing dories, he had two of them built.

Unfortunately the timing and mind-set of the period were wrong. After World War II nearly everybody wanted motorboats. Thus for years there were very few sails seen on the Basin.

In 1948 I sold the *Flying Saucer* to Kelsey Raymond and he renamed her *Mary Lou* in honor of his future wife. That boat taught him to sail and he ventured as far as Sandy Cove in her.

In the twenties and thirties there were always around half a dozen small boats moored off the Harbor View beach. Nearly all of them were open-cockpit sailboats equipped with center-boards because they all lay on the mud at low tide. Originally most of them were a type of sailing dory, gaff-rigged sloops and with lines quite different from the common Lunenburg and Shelburne dories still used by fishermen. I remember that Frank Witherbee and Bob Milbank each had one. These sailing dories had entirely disappeared from the Basin by 1946.

No sail boat here had auxilliary power at that time, either inboard or out-board, and none had a cabin or cuddy. When becalmed, one drifted, anchored, paddled or rowed or one stuck the blade of a knife into the mast or whistled for a breeze.

With no engine or cabin, with only small sailboats, and with the powerful run of the tide and its predictable rise and fall, sailors at that time felt, and actually were, more closely bonded to the elements and more dependent on working in harmony with all the whims and might of Nature than is today's sophisticated sailor with fiberglass hull, roller reefing, cabin and deep-water mooring inside Winchester Point in the mouth of the Bear River or at the new Digby marina. This marina, built in 1995, has been so popular that the facility at Winchester Point was abandoned in 1996.

Many a time in the thirties and forties I have been late for supper, paddled home in a dead calm or anchored by the far edge of the mud and slogged in on foot. Never knowing how a particular sail would end or what conditions would be encountered added a dimension of adventure and surprise that is not present in sailing on the Basin today. Modern large keel sailboats tend to shrink the Basin and lessen the enjoyment—less fun for more bucks.

For protection during hurricanes, small boats were usually sheltered in the Salt Pond at the mouth of the Joggin or behind the Digby government wharf.

An incidental advantage of small boats without deep keels is the ease and cheapness of hauling out and storing over the winter. We made simple cradles using two logs for runners and several crosspieces, including at least one at an angle.

If a cradle were lost or burned up in a bonfire, it was simple to build a new one. A trip at high tide to the beach on Bear Island would net whatever timbers were needed and they could be towed back to the Harbor View beach for assembly.

Beach picnics were common events before World War II. Many of them were clam bakes. For this a ring of stones or gravel, with a gap in its windward side, was made and a large bonfire built in it. When the fire burned down a little, it was covered with a large piece of sheet metal. A layer of fresh, wet rockweed was spread on this, then a bucket of clams spread around, and finally another layer of seaweed on top. None of the broth could be saved this way, but the clams picked up a richer flavor than if steamed in a pot.

Singing and story-telling picked up as darkness fell and often continued until quite late.

The mudflats had not yet been mined and clams were plentiful and easy to dig. The advent of four-wheel drive vehicles and ATVs in the 1980s put an end to that, and now clams are scarce and small.

Aside from steaming and making clam chowder, we used clams for bait when we handlined in the cove or fished from the wharf in Digby. Flounder were plentiful in the cove and occasionally a skate or tom cod was pulled in. Fishing at the Digby wharf then usually produced only harbour pollock.

We often went on picnics and the hotel would put up enormous lunches for us, complete with steaks or chops, frying pans, coffee pots and whatever we ordered for it the night before. Sandy Cove, Point Prim and Bear Island were favorite picnic destinations.

We found that Sandy Cove is more fun at low tide because the firm sand flats are fun to run on and the streams that cross it are perfect for engineering a series of dams and reservoirs. Sandy Cove water was always several degrees colder than that at Smith's Cove, but we would always manage a quick swim nevertheless.

Fishermen were never near the wharf or the numerous fish shacks at Sandy Cove on Sundays. We had great sport then shooting rats with a .22 rifle there as they dashed along their well-trodden runways between shacks. They would take a quick peek out, pull back in and then make a mad dash for it. It was tricky shooting.

Mr. Wilson, the keeper of the Point Prim lighthouse, always had a warm welcome for us. The rugged old wooden structure combined the keeper's dwelling and the lighthouse itself. The light was provided by a single kerosene lamp surrounded by an array of fresnel prisms that focused the light into a beam that was clearly visible from many miles out on the Bay of Fundy. The array of prisms was made to rotate horizontally by means of clockwork run by weights that Mr. Wilson wound up every night with a crank.

The old fog horn at Point Prim was a deep-throated diaphone that gave off an awesome whooooo-ump signal. It came from a horn protruding from its own building that housed a huge gasoline-powered air compressor. Today's thin, high-pitched signal seems anemic to me, as I had come to love the old diaphone.

Beside the diaphone building at the top of the vertical cliff was the hoist used to bring drums of kerosene and other supplies ashore from the lighthouse tender that visited periodically.

The old wooden structure was replaced in 1964 by a boxlike concrete thing with the same vertical red-and-white markings. It is fully automated, but it lacks any esthetic charm whatsoever.

Commercial fishing boats of the twenties and early thirties were small open boats that were divided at the thwarts into several pens or wells. They were narrow and were all powered by "one-lungers," dependable little one-cylinder engines that were started with a pull on the flywheel. They had a distinctive classic bang-bang-bang sound that often included several silent strokes because of non-ignition.

The fishing boats were the right size for one man, and fishermen either set out tubs of trawl with many hooks baited with herring, or they handlined. Those who operated weirs pursed them in by hand and then dipped the herring out with hand nets. It was exhausting work.

Later in the thirties old car engines began to be installed in fishing boats. They were cooled by running a short loop of pipe along the keel, as the fishermen knew that Bay of Fundy water would cool efficiently.

These fishing boats were not subsidized by government grants nor were the weirs. The government did, however, build and maintain wharves, haul-outs and one-cylinder donkey engines used for hauling boats out.

In the late thirties a radically new fishing boat design became popular. It was the Cape Island boat—broad beam, shallow draft aft, high bow, large open cockpit, cuddy forward with wheel and throttle on its after starboard bulkhead, and a roof over the wheel. These were far more seaworthy than the older styles and much more safe and efficient, especially for lobstering.

This design is still in use for lobstering, but now has a cabin instead of a cuddy and an hydraulic gurdy (hoist) near the wheel for hauling pots. The standard size Cape Island boat in moderate weather can carry 50 or 60 pots comfortably in one load.

Before World War II weirs were small and were largely of brush construction. In the sixties weirs became larger, more expensive and more efficient, and required divers to build and maintain them. The new-style weir can be built in deep water, where the bottom is not exposed at low tide.

Up until the ferry wharf was built in the Gut, there was one ferry from Saint John a day. That tied up at the CPR wharf right beside the government wharf. The Princess Helene and her predecessors were not built for passengers to drive their own cars aboard. Instead, employees did it and parked them slowly and laboriously in the hold, driving in over a wide gangplank and entering the ship's side. There were several other gangplanks besides the one used by passengers. At low tide each car was lowered in a painfully-slow elevator to the cargo door in the ship's side.

When the ship arrived from Saint John, the wharf was always crowded and noisy. Men with peaked caps and signs called out the names of their hotels and then drove foot passengers to their destinations. The railway had a siding on the wharf and there was always a chuff-chuff-chuffing steam train there when the ship came in.

The Flett years

In January 1946 Mr. Longmire of Bridgetown offered to buy Harbour View from Gordon Cossaboom for $35,000.

Wartime price controls were still in effect and may have hastened the financial deterioration of the Cossabooms' business. In 1946 the Hotel served full-course lobster dinners for $1.50, and lobster or scallop supper for $1.25. Management requested permission from the government to raise these prices to $2.25 and $1.85 respectively and for steak dinners to $1.50 and steak supper to $1.25. The Hotel served a huge breakfast then for $1.00.

During the early part of Walter Flett's time as owner, Harbour View boasted a band. Dorothy Flett's brother, Ron Longmire, the hotel manager, played the saxophone. Gene Ford, his assistant, played something else and Charles ("Buster") Walker played the drums.

Gene Ford ran the Bingo parties and called out the numbers, introducing such innovations as "crutches" for 77, "clickity click" for 66 and other tricky lingo.

Elliot Odell organized the "Harbour View Follies" around 1964 and many of the summer guests as well as the hotel staff performed an amazing variety of talents one gala night each summer in the Casino. Sally Flett and Nancy Longmire, daughters of the owner and his manager, were great friends and spent many summers here.

Because of the high cost of maintaining the clay tennis court, Flett experimented with a surface of fine slate. This proved unpleasant and unpopular, so when the highway through Smith's Cove was being repaved, he had the paving crew lay a stretch of blacktop on the old court. Its major fault was that it was too short behind the base lines.

With repairs, patches, mumblings and a few twisted ankles, that blacktop served until 1992, when a truly professional all-weather court, with correct dimensions and proper fencing, was built by the Harbourview Cottagers Association.

1954 was a slow year. The Shenstones were in Europe and Whitney J. Oates used their cottage. The only sailboat in the cove belonged to a Mr. Knowlton. Leaman Sarty was doing chores for Mr. Flett. The Longmires had returned to Bridgetown.

Rates in 1958 were still unbelievably low by today's standards:

- Cottages with four or more occupants rented for $7.00 a day per person, including three meals.
- Cottages with fewer than four, $7.50 per person.
- Rooms with bath, double occupancy, $7.50.
- Rooms with running water only, double $6.50, single $7.00.
- Children 6 and under, half rate.

These rates were all American plan: three meals included.

But to put these rates into context, the entire Harbour View property was assessed at $31,200 in 1965, all 120 acres of it as well as all buildings that were not privately owned, and all equipment, bedding, furniture, etc.

The Irvine years

In 1967 Walter Flett, being advanced in years and unwell, and after having operated Harbour View for 22 years, sold it to David and Sylvia Irvine of Cornwall, Ontario. Neither David, a forester (1959 graduate from the University of New Brunswick), nor Sylvia, a registered nurse (Royal Victoria Hospital, Montreal), had had any previous training or experience in the hotel or resort business, but they were young, vigorous and resourceful, and had vision and good taste.

The Irvines arrived with their two-year-old son Geoffrey, who, together with his wife Kelly, now has two children of his own: son Will and daughter Julia.

At that time there still was a staff of 21 at Harbour View, which the Irvines increased to 25. Owners of cottages wondered how it would work out, and whether the property would be turned into a forest or an invalid colony, or both.

The Irvines began by fencing in the pool, switching the pool to fresh water and installing a filtration system; building the children's play-ground; initiating lobster boils and adding four new cottages. Otherwise they operated everything just as Walter Flett had.

Board was $9.00 a day, American plan, children under 10 were half price. There were horses for hire and fresh vegetables came from the hotel garden.

To raise working capital, the Irvines sold the cottage lots to cottage owners when their leases came up for renewal. From then on it was no longer necessary for cottage owners to have their meals at the hotel, and David Irvine built and improved cottage kitchens as requested by the owners and to enhance their attractiveness as rental units.

As many cottages had been transferred to hotel ownership, there were fewer private owners and fewer guests in the hotel dining room. Therefore the Irvines converted #18-19, which was too large to be rented, into a snack bar and named it "Shady Grove." With its hot dogs, potato chips, pop and ice cream cones Shady Grove was a magnet for children and teenagers.

After Shady Grove's activities were shut down, the north end of the building, which had obviously been tacked on at some forgotten time, was removed, placed where the Dodd/Kinsolving cottage had been, position #16, and rented. A few years later #16 was sold to Dr. John (Shirley) Filbee of Halifax.

The remaining portion of Shady Grove, #19, was rented for several years and then sold to Dr. and Mrs. Ian (Margaret) Bruce of Yarmouth. The Bruces often used the cottage on winter weekends for cross-country skiing. In the summer they were there as much as possible with their daughter, Dianna, and son, John.

When Dr. Bruce retired, David Irvine built a storage shed on the north end. Closing in the verandah, building the deck, adding the insulation and the furnace had been done many years earlier, just after the Bruces bought the cottage.

The children's program was begun in 1967, Dave and Sylvia's first year of ownership. Under the leadership of Mona Lou Webb, the program provided child care during the summer months. It began in a rather unstructured way, but became more formal when Nancy Prescesky (now Nancy Irvine) took charge of it in 1973. She took advantage of the full use of the Casino, where there were still reminders of the "Purple Candle Secret," the last band to play at the Saturday night dances.

The only competition for the space in the Casino came from Mrs. Ryno, who dried sheets there on rainy days.

Nancy remembers:

> We had access to a piano, lots of indoor space in the dance area of the building, and some very basic arts and crafts supplies. For three hours every morning and two hours in the evening, the children gathered here for fun and games, arts and crafts, and nature walks. The highlight for the children was our weekly weenie roasts, usually held at the pool. Children from ages four and up were eligible to participate in the program at no extra charge if their parents were vacationing at Harbour View.
>
> There would be from six to twenty children at a time. I ran the program until 1976. Then Arianne Clements, a

former babysitter for the Irvine and Webb children, took over. At the same time, the program was moved to the barn because David Irvine had begun to convert the Casino into the apartment units that were to be renamed Cossaboom Corner.

Arianne ran the program until 1978, at which time my sister, Elisabeth Prescesky, took it over. Elisabeth ran it until it was terminated in 1980.

The program's demise reflected the reduced need for it. The Irvine and Webb children had grown sufficiently to need less supervision, and the cottages were being acquired by private owners.

Now no more than a name and a fond memory, Shady Grove sprang into life in 1969 under the inspired management of Douglas Irvine. He writes about it thus:

Early in the spring of 1969 it was decided by David Irvine that lunches served at the Harbour View Inn were no longer necessary as most of the cottagers had begun eating from their own kitchens. Dave relinquished partial control of cottage #18, which at that time also comprised the central portion of what is currently cottage #16.

The overall plan was to provide a canteen serving lunches and a recreation centre for the growing teenage population of Harbour View. David's youngest brother Douglas (17) and his best buddy Gary Lalonde (18) traveled downstream from Cornwall, Ontario to set up the 'Shady Grove.' The name was borrowed from an album title by an underground musical group called the Quicksilver Messenger Service, from San Francisco (c.1966).

The quaint yet dilapidated cottage, with its surrounding stand of maples, became the perfect hang-out for the very young and old alike. Even the children's program occasionally dropped by, especially when the house band, "Mashed McKann & the Cokemen" (Marshall Webb, Peter Webb and Geoff Irvine) took up positions on the front porch with their homemade instruments. Their early songs were inspired by the laid-back ambiance of The Grove.

Gary took up chef's duties, creating the now legendary Grove Burger (the original quarter-pounder) and the Shady

Dog (a special kind of hot dog with funky striations and oodles of all your favourite trimmings.) For his part, Doug set up and managed the stereo room located within range of the massive beach-stone fireplace, the red card room (divided from the stereo room with yards of boat line and corks suspended from the ceiling), the ping-pong room and the adjoining library. Shady Grove boasted two washrooms and a large bedroom in the back to accommodate the staff.

Outside, the clientele could lounge around at the wooden cable-tables [old wooden spools on which steel dragger cables had been wound] with their faded beach umbrellas, salvaged from a previous Harbour View era. Throughout the day, swimmers would stroll over from the pool and catch a quick bite. A full meal deal could be had for under two dollars.

During the evening, Harbour View staff members, Smith's Cove youths, travelers staying at the nearby trailer park, and of course Harbour View visitors and summer residents could be found drinking super-thick milkshakes and munching on golden fries around the fireplace or out on the porch. Occasionally a concerned parent, or even Dave himself, would drop by to check on things, but of course, everything was always running smoothly.

A belated thanks and a special mention to the MacIntyres, who never complained about the raucous activity, even during wild ping-pong matches between the Harbour View chef, Mark Killam, and Gary Lalonde. These matches were held only a few feet from the MacIntyre's bedroom window.

This summer (1996) the present owners, Marilyn and Gary Copp of Halifax, received the original 'Shady Grove' sign as a cottage-warming gift from Doug, who had managed to keep it under wraps during the previous twenty-five years. Now it's back where it belongs.

In 1971 the Irvines converted the large hotel dining room into four luxurious motel units, and enclosed two sections of the verandah, converting them into dining rooms. They followed this realignment in 1972 by gutting the second floor and rebuilding its five bedrooms so as to include a private bath with each, instead of the preexisting three bathrooms down the hall.

The Irvines operated the dining room for 12 years and then in 1979 sold the hotel business and the building to his sister and brother-in-law, Philip and Mona Webb of Toronto. As the Webbs were in the teaching business, they had the summers off to devote to the really strenuous work of running a country inn. It must have been like a vacation to return to teaching in September.

In 1975 the David and Sylvia Irvine were blessed with a daughter, Jennifer. Jenny was a keen horseback rider and rode extensively in competitions.

Before Jenny was old enough to ride, the Irvines sold the five horses they had kept for renting, but kept Babe. Geoff looked after that gentle old pony and gave pony rides for two summers when he was about twelve. Jenny's horses were strictly her own.

In 1976 the Irvines instituted a Saturday Flea Market. Dealers paid $3 for a table, shoppers paid 25 cents admission.

David Irvine writes about the weekly lobster boils as follows:

> For about five years during the mid to late seventies, Saturday evening lobster boils were staged in the level lawn area beside the pool. All the Hotel staff were given the night off while management—Sylvia and David Irvine and their children, Douglas Irvine, Mona and Philip Webb and their children—cooked the lobster, transported the food to the site, served the guests and cleaned up afterward. The dining room was closed on these evenings while service was delivered to the great out-of-doors.
>
> Tables (which included many recycled wire cable spools), chairs and buffet tables on which to serve the food were set up for Harbour View guests and private cottage owners to enjoy the crustacean delicacies.
>
> Josie Rice's bread and wonderful pies accompanied the lobster and tossed salad, and there were hot dogs and hamburgers for the kids.
>
> Everyone always seemed to enjoy themselves greatly, no doubt due partly to the quality of the food and the company, and partly to the fact that most had attended a cocktail party prior to the event, and went on the enjoy wine and beer with their food. By this time the hotel had become licensed to sell alcoholic beverages and there was no short-

age of good cheer.

One particularly memorable evening began with Eliott 'Pappy' Odell, who was bald as a cue-ball, arriving with a wig in his pocket. To his sister's horror he threatened to don the wig. His sister, Helen Squiers, who absolutely loved lobster, and with whom he shared a quasi love-hate relationship, said she would leave if he put the thing on. Pappy did put it on and Helen, who was in her seventies and rather arthritic, was out of her chair and down the road to their cottage before anyone knew what had happened.

Lynn, Pappy's daughter, later took a plate of lobster to her Aunt Helen, who refused to eat it. However, by the next morning the lobster had mysteriously disappeared from the refrigerator.

Although the lobster boils were a big hit with the private owners, who were loyal supporters, the idea never really caught on with the cottage and hotel guests. No doubt it was one more idea that was a little ahead of its time.

When the Webbs retired from teaching they took up year-round residence in Smith's Cove. They converted the third floor of the Inn into a bright, luxurious apartment and winterized it for their own use.

A new era

In 1988, there being no more cottages owned by the Irvine family business, Harbour View Estate Services Ltd., the Irvines suggested transfer of ownership of the swimming pool, adjacent picnic area, tennis court and children's playground on the corner to the cottage owners.

The owners formed the Harbourview Cottagers Association, sold shares and bought these facilities from the Irvines. The Association hired David Irvine to maintain them and agreed to buy water from him for the pool.

In 1991 the Association installed new play equipment on the playground, and in 1992 had the new tennis court built. No one mourned the passing of the old short court, the treacherous bounces or the rusty chicken-wire backstop except the children who found that lying on the sun-warmed blacktop to be a cozy remedy for a chilling in the pool, but that was much later and not in the Cossaboom era. Now, still much later, sunbathing is not allowed on the new all-weather court.

1993 proved to be a slow year, there being a recession in progress, and both the pool and tennis court were underutilized. That year, Harbour View Estate Services, Ltd. sold vacant land to the owners of several cottages, thereby reducing their stake in Harbour View ownership still further.

The meadow along the shore in front of cottages 14, 16, 18, 20 and 22 was bought as tenants-in-common by the owners of those cottages. The land between cottages 4, 34, 40, 42, Ballentrae and the shore was bought by Hester Bates. The views from all cottages bordering these plots were thus protected.

With the formation of the Harbourview Cottagers Association came the first of several new annual community events since the discontinuation of the Saturday evening lobster boils and the children's program, both of which predated the Webbs' purchase of the Inn. The first new event was the "Pool Party," an annual potluck supper of all members, guests and renters in the level area by the pool. On several occasions it included either a roast pig or roast leg of beef. It is preceded by a softball game for all ages and by numerous games for children. The pool party takes place on the day of the annual general meeting of the Association, usually the first Saturday in August.

The other annual event began in 1995 and has generated much enthusiasm. It is the Harbour View Open tennis tournament, organized and promoted long-distance by Rob and Jenny (Irvine) Begrand of Calgary. This event runs two days on the second weekend in August, and is complete with trophies and appropriately decorated T-shirts and hats.

1995 was dubbed the "Year of the Hooked Rug" by the Nova Scotia Department of Tourism. This spark of an idea fell on dry tinder in Smith's Cove. A number of ladies, both year-round residents of the village and summer people, formed a group that meets weekly in the old Temperance Hall, now the Smith's Cove Museum.

Believe me, they are avid. These ladies not only share a productive craft and produce some exquisite examples of the nearly forgotten art, but they have a marvelous time socially. Meetings always include a brown-bag lunch. In the cold weather they meet in individual members' houses. But should you pass by the Museum around mid-day on a Wednesday and hear gales of laughter drowning out a babble of conversation, you will know the "Smith's Cove Happy Hookers" are in session. Stop in and be royally welcomed.

Progress, be it good or bad, comes with the passage of time. The railway, having gone from being the number one provider of transportation in the Province, continued to lose out to the truck, the bus and the automobile. The DAR was taken over by the CPR and then by the CN. Traffic fell off until there was only one "scooter" (passengers-only) train each day, beginning at Yarmouth in the morning, running up to Halifax, and returning in the evening. It was discontinued the winter of 1990 and the tracks and ties were torn up that summer.

Today the railway right-of-way remains as a scenic route for walking and biking. In the winter it has no equal for cross-country skiing.

The big bridges, such as the ones over the Bear River, the Wolf River at Clementsport, the Sissiboo River at Weymouth and Allain'

Creek at Annapolis Royal are impassible, and the small ones have been torn down. The grade crossings have been paved over, but I still look both ways when I approach one of them.

Harbour View Estate Services, Ltd. further reduced its stake in the colony by selling the water system and the roads along it to Mona Lou and Philip Webb, owners of the Harbourview Inn. David Irvine, being fully occupied with the job of Councilor for the Municipality of Digby, has handed over the job of connecting and winterizing the plumbing in all the cottages to Mike Drucken and no longer takes care of pool maintenance or mowing. In fact, Harbour View Estate Services, Ltd. has discontinued all routine service functions for cottage owners, but concentrates on special construction or renovation projects.

Cabins and their occupants

In the following section the first number [#] corresponds to the traditional way of identifying buildings at Harbour View, and was used on Dr. D. L. Turner's map of 1931. The second number is the actual street locator number according to the system installed in 1992 for use with the 911 emergency system.

#1
Originally Gordon Cossaboom's house, it was built in 1928. It is no longer part of Harbour View.

#2—22 Harbour View Road

The Cossaboom family's house was built in the middle of an apple orchard across from the present Harbourview Inn. It was designed by Clara Cossaboom and built in 1923-4 by William Cossaboom. 1937-1951 it was lived in by Douglas and Mary Cossaboom, then 1951-1967 by the Steadmans, then from 1967 to 1989 by David and Sylvia Irvine.

The Irvines sold it to Philip and Mona Webb, who used it as part of the Harbourview Inn operation. In 1996 Ernest and Rebecca Doucet of Weymouth bought the house to use as their year-round residence They have named the house "Serenity." The Doucet's children are daughter Courtney and son Jeffrey.

#3—25 Harbour View Road

The building, that is now the Harbourview Inn and Cove Restaurant, was known in 1931 as the "Annex," and was built in 1909 to house the overflow from the Hotel. Its architecture copied that of the old Hotel, but before 1938 it lacked a kitchen and dining room. A dining rooth and kitchen were added in the winter of 1938-1939, and the building was then used to replace the old hotel after the fire destroyed it.

#4

This cabin was originally built behind the Cosaboom house (#2) for summer use by Earl Cossaboom. Afterwards it was rented until it was moved to its present location and drastically altered.

The Irvine family had lived year-round in the old Cossaboom house (#2) across the road from the hotel. One summer they sawed the cabin behind it (#4) in half and hauled the two halves down to the beach, thence north along the beach to its present location. They reassembled the cabin on the point where John Sulis had built his original farmhouse.

Because the process was hazardous, anxiety was high until the two house parts were back together. With half the house still on the beach, and with the tide still out, the work day ended and the crew went home for the night. The Irvines scarcely slept that night while they visualized what might happen at the midnight high tide.

For nearly 15 years the Irvines spent summers in the newly reassembled #4 cottage on the point, all the while expanding and remodeling it. In 1989 they moved into it year-round and sold the house on the road (#2) to the Webbs, who divided it into two rental apartments.

The Irvines named their new home *Quince Cottage* because of the large old quince bush that dates back to early Sulis days.

The Irvines' son, Geoffrey, and his wife, Kelly, live in Halifax with their two children, Will and Julia. Daughter Jennifer lives in Calgary with her husband, Rob Begrand.

Quince Cottage has been so transformed that it is unrecognizable as the old #4 cabin. It has been elegantly modernized, expanded and winterized, and equipped with a full finished basement and a large wrap-around deck. The cottage has several out-buildings, including a guest cottage that was formerly a boathouse. The present location is 21 Beachcomber Lane.

#5—59 Harbour View Road

Armstrong cabin in 1931. The Armstrong family came from Windsor, NS. They had two sons, Arthur being the elder. Later the cabin was used as a laundry for hotel linen. It was being used to house male staff members in 1967 when the Irvines arrived, and continued as such until 1979, when it was converted into a convenience

and snack store, and christened "Aunt Minerva's Store." The name was in honor of the first store in Smith's Cove which was operated by Minerva Sulis.

The cabin was then moved up to higher ground across from the playground and bought by Mr. and Mrs. John (Joan) Carling of Halifax. They christened it *Finally*. Stickers from Aunt Minerva's Store still adorn the front window. A large sunny deck has been added to the rear and a lovely garden frames the yard.

In 1994 the Carlings bought the old Gilroy lot (#15, now wooded and without buildings) behind them from David Irvine and are converting it into a woodland garden. An addition is being built on the cottage in 1997.

Carling children: Adam of Halifax, Robin (Mrs. Ken Pineo) of

Chester and Simon, who lives in New York City with his wife, Yvonne.

#6—6 Beachcomber Lane

One of the original 1898 cabins and built of logs. Owned by Rev. Francis Brown of Savannah, Georgia in 1931, but usually rented by the hotel.

When the Irvines arrived in 1967 the cottage was used to house female members of the staff (waitresses and cabin girls). The Irvines tore off the decrepit rear section that hung over the water and was a fire hazard, and added a rudimentary kitchen. It was then rented until 1979 when it was bought by Mr. and Mrs. Michael (Wendy) Emberly of Fall River, NS in 1979. (Emberly children: Mark and Stephen)

The dam that created the duck pond behind #236 and #310 was breached in 1996 and the pond was drained. Gone are the ducks, the frogs and the presence of a sizable body of water for emergency use by firemen. The barn is in the process of being converted into David Irvine's workshop.

#7

Gone. One of the original 1898 log cabins. "Music Box" on 1931 map. Housed four musicians who played in the Harbor View band before World War II.

#8

One of the original 1898 log cabins. Originally rented by the hotel, it was Miss Barnum's cabin in 1931. Miss Barnum was related to the P. T. Barnum of circus fame.

The cabin was moved and attached to #10 (now Langins').

#9—45 Harbour View Road

Casino in 1931. The dance floor could accommodate 150 couples. In 1937 a sunny, 50' x 14' room was added on the south side to serve as a bridge room.

The casino was the site of weekly dances and other social events, such as costume parties, bingo and talks. People came from all over to attend the dances. The canteen at the end of the casino served soft beverages.

As the drinking of alcohol was illegal in public places, it was usually done in cars or in the deep shadows outside. As it was usually done directly from the bottle, the results were occasionally loud or raucous.

Couples often strayed from a dance so as to be more private and more intimate. Several times they came up on our verandah late at night and some grown-up shooed them away. Bishop Waterman, a village resident, campaigned as recently as the seventies for a mercury vapor light to be installed at the chapel to discourage couples from being intimate there on dance nights.

The casino was easy to get into if it was locked. The two chief casino sports for us kids then was sliding on its slippery floor and playing shuffleboard. Nobody seemed to mind how or if we got into the place. The ticket booth on the verandah was made of yellow birch poles and doubled as a jungle gym to climb on.

The original casino burned down in the late 1940s and Flett had it rebuilt on the same site and to the same measurements by carpenters from the French Shore. The dance floor was hardwood and measured 36' by 72'.

The building was operated as a dance hall until the early 1970s. Then for a number of years it served as a rainy-day play site and for the children's program. Afterwards it was down-graded to a storage facility, and the children's program was moved to the barn after the hotel management discontinuing horseback riding.

Finally it was converted to apartments, laundromat and workshop, and named Cossaboom Corner. It was officially opened in its new capacity the summer of 1977 by Nell Cossaboom Steadman.

It is one of the few structures at Harbour View that is still owned by Harbour View Estate Services, Ltd.

#9a

One of two structures torn down before 1931 and not replaced, located between the old hotel and the casino. It had two floors and was quarters for servants.

#9b

The second of the two buildings that were demolished and not replaced. This was a cabin that was occupied by the McClintocks and then by Judge and Mrs. Doggett of Jacksonville, Florida.

#10—10 Beachcomber Lane

One of the original 1898 cabins. Rented as rooms by the hotel, then owned successively by Goodrich and Bostwick. Then completely rebuilt by Ralph Cossitt for Mr. and Mrs. Wilson. It was the Wilson cottage in 1931. Then it was rented by the hotel until bought by Mr. and Mrs. Clifford (Jill) Langin of Halifax (Children: Glen, Holly, Scott).

Before World War II there was a beautiful hedge of double moss roses in front of the cottage. All of it was moved to the Frank Wightman house (bought by Jeff Lindholm in 1996) on the Old Post Road and is still doing well.

My Turnbull grandparents spent the summer of 1947 in #10 but, as it is next to the cemetery, my grandmother, an accomplished watercolorist, didn't like it. "I'll get there soon enough," she said.

The Langins broke with the traditional cottage look by installing a brilliant red steel roof with a fifty-year rating.

#12

Site of original hotel, destroyed by fire in 1938. Before that, farmhouse and home of Charles Sulis. It was added onto several times as the hotel business grew. The children's playground now occupies the site.

See the image on the next page.

The original Harbour View House stood where the playground now is. To the left, between it and the casino, stood a log cabin, possibly the 'Music Box', which housed the young students who were members of the summer band, including former Smith's Cove resident Ben Prince, who played the trumpet.

To the right are the original log cabins that are now owned by the Emberly and Langin families.

#14—70 Harbour View Road

Leahy cottage in 1931. Arthur and Ethel Leahy lived in Roland Park, Maryland with their two sons: Norton and Hamilton. Arthur's brother was Admiral Leahy of WW II fame.

The cabin was lived in briefly by the Dodds. Then it was rented by the hotel for several summers until it was purchased in 1977 by Bishop and Mrs. Stuart (Frances) Wetmore of Millbrook, New York. The Wetmores named it *Wetmore Place*. Up until, 1995 Frances Wetmore hosted a show of paintings by Harbour View artists each August. The paintings were hung on the fence to the north of the swimming pool. Frances Wetmore and daughter-in-law Rebekah are artists.

The Stuart Wetmore children: Nancy, Mary (Mrs. John Bohun), Andrew (and Rebekah), Edward ("Ted" and his wife, Barbara) and Robin. The Andrew Wetmore children: Caleb, Helen and Elizabeth. Mary's children are Nicholas and Jennifer. Nancy's children are Alexander, Jeremy and Malcolm. Robin's son is Jason. Ted's children are Robert and Karen.

#15

Site now vacant. Cabin built for Mrs. Beatrice Gilroy in 1917 by Ralph Cossitt. Mrs. Gilroy was living there in 1931. Miss Anna Burns stayed with her in the role of quasi-adopted daughter and protégée, and raised an exuberant flower garden, her sweet peas being the biggest hit.

Miss Burns inspired many neighbors to improve their gardens and was active in all horticultural events in the area. Mrs. Gilroy was a tall elderly woman with white hair piled on top of her head. One day she asked Mr. Cossitt to build her an "elevator." He scratched his head and tried to visualize how an elevator could be used in that one-storey cabin.

When pressed for details Mrs. Gilroy explained that the "elevator" was in fact a clothes pole, something with a crotch or hook at the top to support and elevate the middle of a loaded clothes line. (What child of the 1990s knows what a clothes pole is?)

After Mrs. Gilroy's time Garnet Adams of Smith's Cove, a younger brother of Lloyd and Lillian Adams, lived in that cabin for a year and afterwards sold it to Mr. Tatem of Puerto Rico. When the Cossabooms refused to sell the land under the cabin to him, Mr. Tatem had the cabin moved up the Old Post Road to where it stands opposite Mrs. Edith McClearn's house. It is now owned by Barbara Davis of Halifax.

The land on which the cabin stood is now part of the Carling property.

#16—76 Harbour View Road

Built about 1903 for Mr. and Mrs. Kaunt. Located between the Lord cottage (#18) and the Leahy cottage (#14). In 1931 it belonged to Mr. and Mrs. Dodd from Brookline, Massachusetts.

Mrs. Dodd was a sweet little doll of a lady. Mr. Dodd had an equine face with huge gray eyebrows and a cowcatcher moustache to match, in both size and color. He spoke only seriously and never smiled. Perhaps it was the high, stiffly starched collar and prickly tweed jacket that he always wore that made him that way. He had a brown mole the size of a dime on his left cheek. I think he was shy, or didn't know how to relate to children because I can only remember his profile.

The Dodd's chauffeur was a jovial gent named simply Taylor. Taylor had a gold watch chain with an American five dollar gold piece on it. He and I were great pals. Taylor, like the other chauffeurs who were from "away", slept at Knolltop (#43).

The Dodd's nephew, Lewis Perry of Brookline, MA, was a frequent visitor and a great pal of Bob Milbank.

In 1939, after the Dodds were no longer able to come to Smith's Cove, the Rev. and Mrs. Ovid (Alma) Kinsolving of Summit, New Jersey bought their cottage. Mr. Kinsolving also bought a wooded lot across the road from Sunnymeade (our cottage, #22) and spent most of his time that summer clearing the front half of it. Their son, Pitt, helped with the clearing in 1940 and 1941.

The Kinsolving cottage was in such bad condition that Mr. Flett refused to renew the land lease at any price. He considered the building beyond repair and a hazard to the community. The Kinsolvings planned to build a new cabin on the cleared land, but never did.

During World War II, Rev. Kinsolving bought the adjacent wooded lot to the north of the first lot from his cousin, Louise Jaggar, and cleared some of that land in 1945 and 1946. Ovid and Alma Kinsolving both died before the clearing was finished. The cottage then reverted to hotel ownership and was torn down.

Pitt Kinsolving, the owner of both lots, lives in Pasadena, California. Pitt visited Smith's Cove in 1996, having ridden the whole round trip on his motorcycle.

Part of #18 was removed and converted into a cottage on the Kinsolving lot (#16). It was bought by Dr. Filbee of Halifax, and several years later he sold it to Mr. and Mrs. Edward McAniff of New York City, who named it Eagle's Nest.

Mr. McAniff was the retired Chief of the New York City fire department. The McAniffs conveyed the property to their daughter Diane and son-in-law Harold Clapp of Bear River.

Diane's children: daughter Christian Anson and son Samuel Anson, both of California. The Clapps have sold their home in Bear River and spend much of their time in southern waters on their cruising ketch.

#17—77 Harbour View Road
Built in 1912 for Mr. and Mrs. Roome (pronounced "Rome") of New York.

The Roomes had a lovely flower garden built around a small pond bor-dered with Japanese irises and cattails. Many of the ornamental trees can still be seen. The Roomes had a bowling green behind their house.

Their daughter Elizabeth had a German governess and was a great friend of Isabel Cossitt in the early twenties. Elizabeth was known for the fur piece she wore around her neck in July and August.

In 1931 the cottage was owned by Mrs. Louise G. Roome. Afterwards it was owned briefly by F. M. Graves and then by Dr. Rapp. Then it was owned by the hotel.

The cottage, which was difficult to rent because it had no view of the Basin, was bought by Dr. And Mrs. Nuri (Olive) Birsel of Digby in 1971. They built a room between the cottage and the garage, thus connecting

17

the two buildings and converting the garage into living space. The Birsel children are Robert, Suzanne, Marcus and Kate.

The Birsels also bought a piece of land up the hill between #34, #40 and #42. As of 1996 this land has never been built on. At the same time they bought a parcel of land adjoining the cemetery, #4c (old location) and the beach, but which had never been a part of Harbour View.

In 1980 the Birsels sold the cottage to Mr. and Mrs. Christopher (Mary Ellen) Hopgood of Halifax. The Hopgood children are Jane, Geoffrey and Sarah. They named the cottage Linden Cottage because of the fragrant linden trees planted by the Roomes and that still line the driveway.

Lee and Victoria Harwood of Halifax bought the cottage in 1996. They have three daughters: Amanda, Lauren and Alexandra.

#18—82 Harbour View Road

Built 1901(?). Mr. John B. Lord of Scarsdale, New York owned it in 1931. Mr. Lord and his son Bright were keen sailors. The cottage was later owned by the McLennons.

Mr. Lord erected a flagpole in the field below the cottage and ran up the Stars and Stripes. Some people objected because it was not accompanied by the Canadian flag. After much discussion, Mr. Lord added a yard arm, to one end of which he hoisted the red Canadian ensign and to the other the American flag. To the masthead above them both, he ran the Union Jack. Everybody was happy.

Each morning he conducted his own ceremony, sounding "colors," American style, on his bugle and running up all three flags. "Colors" again at sunset when all three flags were put to bed. He kept an enormous megaphone his verandah wall through which he used to bellow for me to come and help him with the halyards and the proper folding of the flags. I usually tried to be somewhere else at those times.

Today the base of the flagpole remains and puzzles visitors. For a few years Dr. Bruce planted marigolds around it as though in memory of something or someone departed—the "Bruce Memorial." Time and the elements will eventually reduce it to its original components.

Mr. Lord further distinguished himself by dying in the dining room. He did it at dinner on a hot Sunday. He simply slumped in his chair and six men carried him out the back door.

Six men were more than were needed because he was of slight build and average height. But there were six men who were eager to get in on the act and they carried him out like pall bearers and laid him on the grass in the shade of some shrubbery.

I was older by that time and was sitting at our usual table by the back door. Word buzzed around the dining room that Mr. Lord had fainted, and we went on eating, but more quietly than before.

Mr. Lord always dressed in a white shirt, white trousers, white shoes, small black bow tie, white Panama hat with a narrow black ribbon on it and pince-nez glasses on a black ribbon. He kept a canoe on his verandah and occasionally paddled it alone out to Bear Island. Mr. and Mrs. Longmire stayed in this cottage during the Flett years.

Dr. and Mrs. Ian (Margaret) Bruce of Edinburgh, Scotland bought the cottage from the hotel. They named the cottage *Imbertville*. Children: Dianna (Mrs. Dianna Bruce-Wootton of Dumfriesshire, Scotland) and John (married to Shelly) of Ottawa. John has one son. Diana has a son and a daughter

Mr. and Mrs. Gary (Marilyn) Copp of Halifax bought the cottage in 1996. The Imbertville sign is gone and the original Shady Grove sign hangs in its place. The Copps have added a deck and cut back some of the maples that had begun to hide and damage the cottage.

#19

Site wooded and vacant except for a well. This was the site of the Ward cabin in 1931, which was occupied by Mrs. Ward of Washington, DC. A Mrs. Jaggar (not the bishop's wife) stayed with her.

Mrs. Ward so closely resembled Mrs. Herbert Hoover that Washington policemen, on duty directing traffic, would stop all other cars and wave her through. She never complained about it.

After Mrs. Ward's time, Ross Bell, a Smith's Cove carpenter, lived in the cottage one winter. It was then moved down to replace the Seixas cottage (#20), which had been demolished because it was considered unsafe and too expensive to repair.

The lot where the Ward cottage stood was sold to Dr. And Mrs. Ian (Margaret) Bruce, then of Yarmouth and now of Edinburgh, Scotland. They sold the lot in 1993 to Christopher Hopgood.

#20—88 Harbour View Road

Built about 1906. Seixas cottage in 1931. First owned by Mr. Nash (of Tiffany Glass), then by

Mr. Irvins (not Irvine).

The cottage then belonged to Mr. Seixas from Mexico, who had his daughters Sybil and Mavis with him. They were all ardent tennis players. Afterwards it was owned by the hotel and rented, and finally torn down and replaced by moving #19 to the site in 1954.

This was rented for years by Winnifred ("Winnie") Cossaboom McIntyre until Mr. and Mrs. James (Ann) MacLean of Halifax bought it. The MacLeans named tha cottage *Tigh Na Mara*, meaning "View of the Sea" in Cape Breton Gaelic. (The name never stuck.) The MacLeans enclosed the verandah and built on a deck.

The MacLean children are Tricia, Jamie and Stephen John.

They sold the cottage in 1991 to Jane Lessel, also of Halifax.

#22—94 Harbour View Road. *Sunnymeade*

Built for my grand-mother, Mrs. Caroline Hanson of East Orange, New Jersey by Ralph Cossitt in 1928 on the site of the original casino. The old casino had been built in 1910 of vertical logs and caulked with moss, and had fallen into dis-repair.

During our second summer at Harbor View, Nanny (Mrs. Hanson) leased the lot where the old casino was being torn down. My mother drew the floor plan of the cottage and Mr. Cossitt spent a long time telling her that he could not build it because he couldn't design a roof to fit it. After he scratched his head enough, he agreed to build it anyhow.

It stands today (1996) much as it was built. The white cedar shingles on the sides are still the originals.

Mr. Cossitt's ingenuity will become apparent when you study the roof. On the road side there are three sections that go up to a common ridge-pole, two of one pitch, the center one of a steeper pitch. On the Basin side there is a central gable with a roof on either side of it. The pitch of those roofs become less steep as the sections go out over the ends of the large verandah. The center section of the verandah roof has at least three different pitches to it.

Not long before building Sunnymeade, Mr. Cossitt built a large cottage for Dr. and Mrs. Daniel Turner of Norfolk, Virginia (later owned and occupied by Mr. and Mrs. Walter Flett, now by Mrs. Audrey Charman of Halifax) and Nanny admired many of its features. One in particular was Mr. Cossitt's use of clear, unfinished, tongue-and-groove Douglas fir to sheathe the interior walls and ceilings.

This wood was produced in British Columbia and was horribly expensive compared with the native spruce flooring and the rough, unplaned native spruce of which the rest of the cottage was built. As a compromise to cost, Nanny ordered her bedroom, the guest room and the bathroom between them to be sheathed with Douglas fir. There would be a certain economy to this, she argued, because the walls between the bathroom and the two bedrooms need be only the thickness of a single board, the board being planed and finished equally well on both sides, and it would be a shame to hide either side of it. Mr. Cossitt advised against the thin walls, but he built them just the same.

Mr. Cossitt was the master builder of Harbor View. He built the Odell cottage (still owned by granddaughter Lynn Odell), the Blackett cottage (now Harper), the new casino (converted by David Irvine in 1977 into apartments, laundromat and workshop), the Mathers' cottage (now Fitches'), the birch (St. Anne's) chapel and many others. He made repairs or alterations on every structure in the community and his skill, style and dependability were admired by everybody.

Sunnymeade was conveyed to Mrs. Hanson's daughter, Mrs. W. Wallace (Marjorie) Turnbull, then to Marjorie's son, Charles, and his wife Priscilla.

Wallace died in 1964, and in 1972 Marjorie married Arthur Brentano of Sarasota, Florida. Ownership later went to Charles and Priscilla's children, Linda, David and Wendy. It is now owned by David and Wendy.

This is one of three cottages in the Harbour View colony that have been in continuous ownership of the same family.

It is now being enjoyed by Caroline Hanson's great-great grandchildren: Laura and Lindsay McCarthy; Elizabeth, Douglas and Caroline Turnbull; and Emily and Amy Spielmann.

A sundeck was added in 1957 and removed in 1980. Since 1982 the Turnbulls have run their own vegetable garden every summer, arriving in mid-May to plant it.

Bob Milbank wrote the following about my father, W. Wallace Tumbull:

> He was tall, very handsome, gentle, kind, imaginative, resourceful, inquisitive, and ready-to-go. However, in the 1920s his children were not old enough to provide much companionship or to keep up physically with some of the projects he had in mind. That is how I lucked out. I was ten years older than Charles.
>
> Once he wanted to motorboat over and explore the Victoria Beach area, so he invited me to go with him. It was an all day trip and he took water and food for lunch. We heated water for tea and I learned to drink it without lemon or milk, only sugar. He said he liked it that way, not that he had forgotten lemon or milk, and I liked it too.
>
> Another time he invited me to go trawl fishing on St. Mary's bay with regular, full-time fishermen. They had an open motorboat, about 25 feet long, loaded with bushel baskets containing coiled trawl line.
>
> Half a mile out we anchored the end of the trawl with a floating buoy attached to it. From there we went slowly while one man payed out the trawl, one basket at a time. At 6 foot intervals along the trawl there was a 3 foot leader with a baited hook on it. Altogether the trawl must have been about a mile long. One of the fishermen attached an anchor and buoy to that end and dropped it.
>
> Back at the first buoy we had hot coffee and a roll, and relaxed for a while. Then they restarted the engine, pulled up the anchor and buoy and began to pull in the trawl. I was amazed; there was something on every hook, mostly flounder, cod, halibut and other edible fish, but also dogfish, sea cucumbers, ugly sea robins, and scallops.
>
> I was taught how to open the scallop and pull out and throw away all but the little round muscle attached to the middle of each shell. They were easy to cut loose with the sharp edge of the other half of the shell, and they were

sweet, tender and delicious.

#24—102 Harbour View Road

Milbank cottage in 1931. Built in 1910 by Ralph Cossitt for Mr. and Mrs. Harold (Edith) Milbank. The Milbanks, their daughters Edith ("Babe") and Barbara, and son, Bob, were our neighbors to the north.

In the late thirties the cottage became hotel property and was rented. A family named Ritchie summered there in 1959. At another time the Molsons rented it.

Hugh and Judy Smith of Halifax bought the cottage in 1976 and enjoyed it for many summers with their five children: Whipple, Amy, Jamie, Victoria and Katie. The Smiths removed the roof from the north end of the verandah, thus converting that part of it into a deck. They also added skylights to brighten the interior.

Hugh's parents, Dr. and Mrs. Ralph (Pat) Smith had stayed at Harbor View in 1946. A radiologist, Dr. Smith was then working at HMCS Cornwallis in Deep Brook. The Ralph Smiths rented various cottages at Harbour View. They also have a daughter, Barbara Wil-kins of Newfoundland. Dr. Smith died in 1966.

In 1986 Hugh and Judy Smith sold their cottage to Dr. and Mrs. Stanley (Carol) Nelson of New York City, who already owned the one just to the north of it (#26). The Nelsons used #24 for guests and for their children, and stayed in #26 themselves.

The Nelsons enjoyed tennis, but their interest in Nova Scotia waned. They did not come up in 1995 or 1996.

In 1997 they sold the cottage to David and Susan Turnbull of suburban Boston. Children: Elizabeth, Douglas and Caroline.

#26—104 Harbour View Road

Built in 1910 for Mr. Frederick S. ("Papa") Little of New York, who owned it until he died in 1950.

Being lame, Mr. Little walked with a cane. He was one of the most charming men I have ever known and a friend to all Harbor View people. Everyone called him "Papa." He was Mrs. Edith Milbank's father.

Papa and his son-in-law, Harold Milbank, built adjoining cabins (24 and 26) the year after Harold and Edith were married.

Mr. Little's son, Duncan, and daughter-in-law Dorothy, also of New York City and later of Ronkonkoma, Long Island, stayed with him for much of every summer. They were both devoted amateur photographers and were among the first non-commercial movie photographers.

Duncan MacDougal Little often showed up at formal occasions in a kilt and full highland regalia.

One summer while the cottage was owned by the hotel and rented, it narrowly escaped a serious fire. A mentally handicapped young man under the supervision of his counselor put hot ashes into a garbage bag and placed it on the porch. The problem was detected before it could get out of control.

The hotel owned the cottage until 1975, when it was sold to Stan and Carol Nelson. Nelson children: Bruce, Andrew, Robert, and Jandy.

In 1997 the cottage was bought by Grant and Pam (Prescesky) Stonehouse of Tantallon, NS. The Stonehouse children are son Aaron and daughter D'Arcy.

#27—92 Jaggar Lane. *Tall Trees*

Built 1920(?) for Dr. and Mrs. Daniel (Alma) Turner of Norfolk, Virginia on land purchased from Bishop Jaggar, and therefore technically not originally a part of Harbour View. It was sold by the Turner estate to Mr. and Mrs. Walter W. (Dorothy) Flett for use as their summer home while they owned the hotel.

Then the Fletts sold it to Dr. Jack (Audrey) Charman of Halifax. It is now owned by Mrs. Audrey Charman.

Charman children: David Charman and Judy MacLellan, who take turns staying in the cottage every summer with their spouses and children. Peter and Judy MacLellan's children are Scott, Jamie and Allison. David and Doreen Charman's children are John, Kevin, Sam and Caitlin.

#28—114 Harbour View Road

Built 1923 for the Byrne sisters, Molly and Alice, and their brother, Oswald. Their cottage had special kind of front yard, the side away from the street. It slopes down steeply away from the cottage and was then densely covered with large spruce trees with no undergrowth. The lower branches of the trees had

been removed and the ground underneath was smooth and covered with a layer of slippery spruce needles. The slope was so slippery that we children could ski down it with no more than our leather-soled shoes.

The house itself was unique, also. It had a downstairs suite of three small rooms that were accessible only from outdoors. It was a strange structure that was added on as an afterthought. There were no stairs leading to it and it appeared to cling to the long posts that held up the rest of the cottage. That was Oswald's quarters.

The fireplace in the living room is in the corner and faces in, making it and the full length of the chimney stand at 45 degrees to the eaves.

The Byrnes had a lively cocker spaniel that dashed in the kitchen door one day and ran straight through the house, out onto the verandah, out into the void beyond and hit the ground more than a full storey below. He died instantly.

In the late twenties, this cabin was rented to William S. and Julia L. Adams of New York City. Julia was Papa Little's niece. They had four children: Caswell (later a well-known sports writer for the New York *Herald Tribune*), Lois, Billy and Barbara.

For many years Dorothy Bell and Jane Runyon, both members of the faculty of Bradford Junior College owned the cottage. Because the road ran within five or six feet of the cottage, causing a dust and noise problem and limiting privacy, the Irvines relocated the road to its present position some sixty feet distant.

The cottage was then bought by Ken and Julie Sobol of Montreal. Ken was an author of children's books and later a TV writer.

The Sobols sold the cottage to Bill and Lorna Mahar of Halifax. Bill Mahar sold it in 1992 to Ms. Hannah ("Honey") Shields of New York City. Honey cleared the dense spruce thicket to the northeast, thus opening a view of the Basin.

Honey's Mouse House is what Honey has named the place, no doubt in recognition of her silent tenants.

#30—122 Harbour View Road

Built 1903. Owned first by people named Shipman. Bought in 1927 by Mr. and Mrs. Caswell (Virginia) Barrie of Scarsdale, New York, who added on the south wing. Mrs. Barrie was Harold Milbank's sister.

I often played at the beach with their young daughter Virginia ("Virginia Junior"), although she was younger than I. I was in awe of Mr. Barrie because he had a "wooden" leg, having lost the real one in a car accident in 1936.

Mr. Barrie bought many locally-made hooked rugs and exported them to the US. Many years later, daughter Virginia married James Squiers, son of Helen Odell Squiers and grandson of Mrs. Louise Odell (the first owner of #44), who had also spent many childhood summers at Harbor View, but who had not met Virginia until 1947.

Ada Winchester was cabin girl for the Barries and Billy Roop was their chauffeur. They kept their Packard car in the garage just south of the pump house. That garage held half a dozen cars, but was torn down in the late thirties.

In 1936 or 1937, the Barries sold the cottage to Mr. Laird of Toronto, who summered here with his daughters, Diana and Daphne. One of them was a keen tennis player, as was her father. The other daughter, a painter, was crippled.

Then the hotel owned and rented the cottage until it was bought by two couples: Ron and Marilyn Jolemore and John and Marilyn Corbett, all of Halifax. (Jolemore son: Shawn. Corbett children: Mark and Karla.)

The Jolemores sold their interest in the cottage in 1995. It is now owned by John Corbett and his son, Mark.

#32—124 Harbour View Road

Witherbee cottage in 1931. Built ca. 1903. Owned by Mr. and Mrs. Frank (Mary) Witherbee of San Diego, California, having retired there from Boston.

I was very fond of them both. Mr. Witherbee had snow-white, curly hair and a little moustache to match. He was very tan. He was a keen golfer and sailor.

After the Witherbees' time the cottage reverted to hotel ownership until Mr. Tatem of Puerto Rico bought it in 1946 or 1947. He remodeled it extensively.

Then again the hotel acquired it. In 1966 Lloyd Adams was burning grass in the field below the hill on which #32 sits, when the fire flashed out of control and raced up the hill to wipe out the cottage. The cottages on either side of it could just as easily have been destroyed also.

Douglas and Nancy Irvine of Hantsport, NS have built a large and elegant concrete walk-out basement on the site, where they and their children, Dylan and Nataleah, spend the summer. They plan eventually to built a conventional first floor above it.

Because of its unusual construction, they have named the place *Duck Downs*, but this is no reflection upon its headroom, as the minimum ceiling height is 8 feet, but as much as 11 feet high in several rooms.

125 Harbour View Road

Pump house and well. The pump was originally powered by a windmill. By the mid-1920s an electric pump raised water into an elevated tank.

The well is 40 feet deep and contains five feet of water, but it is sufficient to supply most of

The pump house, renovated and no longer crooked.

the Harbour View colony, including enough water to fill the swimming pool and keep it filled all summer. This is remarkable because the well is located on the highest point of land at Harbour View.

#34—142 Harbour View Road

The Dodds, then residents of Newton, Massachusetts, built this cottage in 1910 and sold it to Miss Estelle Ogden of Boston five years later. Preferring to be closer to the hotel because of poor heath, the Dodds bought #16.

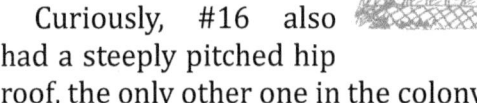

Curiously, #16 also had a steeply pitched hip roof, the only other one in the colony.

Miss Ogden was a dear, little, unattractive lady who wore her white hair on the top of her head in a bun. She was a generous soul who sponsored many causes and who was one of the chief contributors to the construction of the Birch Chapel.

She had a special place in her heart for Kelsey Raymond, whom she measured every year on her doorpost. The penciled measurements are still there.

Miss Ogden's chauffeur was Donald, the youngest of the Cossaboom sons. Miss Ogden left enough money to Donald when she died for him to build a house up on Sunset Hill.

Miss Simpson, a devoted companion to Miss Ogden, was a wonderful cook. She made legendary cookies and doughnuts in Miss Ogden's rudimentary kitchen and served them daily with mid-morning coffee and mid-afternoon tea.

Before marrying Cecil Raymond and becoming Kelsey Raymond's mother, Nan Cossaboom cleaned the cottage and made the beds for Miss Ogden.

Kelsey Raymond remembers being taken by Miss Ogden to distribute candy to the children in Jordantown. Miss Ogden and Miss Simpson used to visit the Raymonds in New York City in the winter.

Miss Ogden died in 1938 and bequeathed the cottage to her niece, Phoebe G. (Mrs. Edward L.) White of Adelphi, New Jersey. Phoebe died in 1946 or early in 1947, and her son "Neddie," Edward L. Jr. of Freehold, New Jersey, inherited the cottage.

Phoebe's widower, Col. Edward L. White, died on board the ship from Boston to Yarmouth in 1948 and "Neddie" gave the cottage to

Blanche Woodman, who had cleaned the cottage for many years.

Blanche sold the cottage to Hester (Mrs. Mills) Fries of Montclair, New Jersey in 1949. The Frieses and their sons, Russell, Barry and Billy, enjoyed the place until Mills Fries died in 1959.

Mrs. Fries married Col. John Bates of Maplewood, New Jersey in 1962. She bought the land on which the cottage stands in 1970 and the land between it and the Basin in 1993.

Hester Mount Bates's mother was Allen Shenstone's sister. Therefore Michael Shenstone and Hester are first cousins. Hester formerly played top quality tennis and golf.

Colonel Bates died in 1995, and Hester Bates now owns the cottage.

#36

This cabin was built for Mr. Percival Howe, a New York lawyer. He also owned a fishing and hunting camp back on Sporting Lake. The stained-glass window over the altar in the chapel is in Mr. Howe's memory ("who fell asleep in 1927").

#36 became the Chapman cabin in 1931. Soon afterwards it was torn down. The concrete foundation posts can still be seen on the Bates land.

#38

Built 1908 or 1911 for Mr. and Mrs. Chard. It was owned by the Chards in 1931. Mrs. Chard was an artist from New York City. The hotel owned the cabin after Mrs. Chard and rented it.

The cottage had a high ceiling and a mezzanine. The wooden structure was torn down, but the chimney still stands and is in remarkably good condition. The charcoal on the ground around it indicates either that the cottage was burned down or that there have been fires in the fireplace after the cottage was gone.

The site is now overgrown with trees and myrtle and is sometimes referred to as *Hidden Hearth.* Children believe that "Little People" live there. (A grown-up walking in there alone would have no trouble thinking about "Little People" either.)

For several years in the 1970s the area in front of the hearth was kept cleared except for the carpet of myrtle. A trail with an arch over its entrance and the sign "Chard's Grove" led to it.

#39—150 Harbour View Road. St. Anne's Chapel

The chapel was built in 1918-19.

Although the Anglican community of Harbour View and the surrounding area has shrunk, services are held in the chapel every Sunday during the summer. Perhaps more visitors are attracted to the chapel now to see an exquisite example of rustic architecture than to worship formally. People still come from afar to see the birch chapel with its unique rustic simplicity and creative use of unpeeled yellow birch poles for trim. It is a favorite place for weddings, and plaques on the walls speak of devoted and beloved pilgrims to Harbour View of former summers.

Construction on St. Anne's ("Birch") chapel began the day the Armistice was signed, November 11, 1918 and was completed in time for dedication the first Sunday in July 1919. The land was donated by William Cossaboom and the building itself cost between $2500 and $3000.

Miss Austin, the Smith's Cove postmistress, played the organ during most of the Flett years. Later on Mrs. Tiffin Shenstone was the organist. Today the rector, Rev. Ron Evans, doubles as minister and organist, and shuttles between St. Anne's and his other charges: St. Matthew's in Deep Brook and St. Edward's in Clementsport.

A large boulder in front of the door bears a plaque in memory of John Andrew Richardson, DD, Archbishop of Fredericton, 1868-1938.

Inside the chapel are many more memorial plaques: Caroline T. Hanson, 1865-1953; Adele Dixon Little, died 1929; Frank Norton, died 1930; Sara Frances Norton, died 1930; W. Wallace Turnbull, 1896-1964; Terry Guy Adams, 1954-1972; Olive M. Paxton, 1923-1972; Percival Spurr Howe, died 1927; Locke Tiffin Shenstone 1901-1987; Molly Shenstone 1897-1967; Helen Odell Squiers, 1896-1985; Allen Goodrich Shenstone, 1893-1980; Katherine Harper Meade, 1929-1983; Ralph E. Cossitt, 1879-1971, warden and church officer for 52 years; May Turnbull; The Ven. Archdeacon Fortin, DD, died 1927; Frank Bernard Witherbee, died 1938; William Minor Cossaboom, 1873-1927; Bradford Boardman, killed in WW I, 1918; Charles M. Bostwick, Jr., killed in WW I, 1870-1917.

#40—8 Chapel Lane

Built ca. 1920. Wylshire cottage in 1931.

The Hon. Pat (Margaret) Missick of Bermuda rented it in the 1960s. They were famous for the miniature Austin that they kept in Nova Scotia and for their marathon bridge games.

Mr. and Mrs. Russell (Cathy) Boyle of Dartmouth are its present owners. Russell, also a bridge devotee, plays in tournaments across Canada. The Boyles enclosed the verandah and added a deck.

Children: Jennifer, Cindy and Matthew.

#41—11 Chapel Lane

The first Argonaut Knoll building. Built originally of horizontal whole logs for Charles F. Chase, owner of Argonaut Knoll. Known as *Pioneer* cabin in 1931.

Originally there was a flagpole in front of the cabin on which only one flag flew: that of the U.S.A.

In contrast to the transformation of *Knoll Top*, *Pioneer* remained substantially the same style until 1992. The well and windmill behind the building supplied water to all Argonaut Knoll cabins. The windmill was still there in 1946, but was no longer operating.

David Irvine renovated the interior of *Pioneer* before selling it to Ann and Carl Boswick of Halifax. They had two sons.

In 1991 the Boswicks sold it to the Harper children, Anne (Mrs. Joseph Gajewsky), Malcolm (whose wife is Kara Kritif Harper), Claire and Jeanne. It needed major repairs (front and back sills, chimney work and wiring) when the Harpers bought it, but they have remodeled it and made it safe and livable.

It now sports new cedar-shingle siding and a curved deck that is not in keeping with the original design, but is attractive and practical.

#42—20 Chapel Lane

Blackett cottage in 1931. Built 1920(?) by Ralph Cossitt for the Blackett family.

It reverted to hotel ownership and was bought by Dr. And Mrs. Birsel. They retained the lot to the south of it and sold the cottage to the Grasso family of Massachusetts.

After five or six years the Grassos sold it to Mr. and Mrs. Donald (Sylvia) Harper of South Hamilton, Massachusetts. The cottage is now owned by Mrs. Sylvia Harper of Rockport, Massachusetts.

#43—6 Cottage Lane

The original *Knoll Top* was built in 1909. This was formerly the most important building on Argonaut Knoll.

Guests at the original Argonaut Knoll took all their meals at Harbor View House and paid $6 a week for full board.

The building was built of logs had two storeys and verandahs all the way around upstairs and down, with an outside stairway connecting them.

Knoll Top was only important to us children on rainy days. Then we would gather there and play tag, and run round and round the balconies.

Ralph Cossitt tore *Knoll Top* down in the late thirties because it was unsafe and not feasible to repair.

Walter Flett had a very small cottage built on the site around the original fireplace and chimney. He called it Honeymoon Cottage because of its size.

The Irvines sold this to Rev. and Mrs. Mike (Donna) Coram of High Point, North Carolina. The Corams had the cottage expanded and renovated, and added a deck with a superb view.

It is now the summer home of Mrs. Donna Coram of Woodbridge, Virginia. She has restored its original name, but spells it *Knolltop.*

#44—28 Cottage Lane. *Seagull Cottage*

Built for Mrs. Louise Odell in 1916 by Ralph Cossitt.

Visiting the Smith's Cove summer home of her friend, Mrs. Melendy of Tarrytown, New York, Mrs. Odell fell in love with the area. She had previously summered in Scotland, but found New Scotland equally to her liking and much more convenient.

Her husband was an Episcopal minister in Portland, Maine who rarely came to Smith's Cove. Later he was chaplain at Sing Sing prison in New York state. Mrs. Louise Odell also lived in Tarrytown, NY. She played the organ at St. Anne's chapel before Miss Jaggar did. She also directed a children's choir there.

Mrs. Richardson and Mrs. Odell were great friends. Mrs. Richardson came down one time from Fredericton, NB to visit Mrs. Odell in Tarrytown, NY. Mrs. Odell by that time was no longer able to use the stairs. She was watching for Mrs. Richardson from her seat by an upstairs window and sent the maid downstairs to let her in when she saw her arrive.

Only minutes later, by the time her guest was shown up to see her old friend, Mrs. Odell was dead.

Mrs. Odell's son, Elliot, inherited the cottage in the early 1940s, but her daughter, Mrs. Helen Squiers, continued to stay there every summer (except during the war years) until her death. She spent part of each of nearly seventy summers at Seagull Cottage. Elliot married three times and had no interest in Harbour View until he married his third wife, Van Davis Odell, Lynn's mother.

David Irvine renovated the one-car garage in 1974 to house Mrs. Squiers when her brother was in residence. David named it HOSA (Helen Odell Squiers Annex).

Upon Elliot's death in 1977 Elliot and Van's daughter, Lynn Odell of Bedford, NY, inherited the cottage. She is the present owner.

In the mid 1950s Elliot found the Odell coat of arms at Fort Anne and began tracking the family history. Eventually an ancestor was found who had settled in Smith's Cove in 1792. There was no previous knowledge of this connection.

In 1975 the back porch was enclosed and converted into a breakfast room.

The name of the cottage remains the same, but Lynn has named the site Loon Landing because of her fascination for those birds that are so prevalent in her vicinity. She rents the cottage to Barbara and Jim Wilkins of Newfoundland in July (Barbara is Hugh Smith's sister) and to John and Annette Marshall of Halifax in August. The Marshall children are Heather and Charles.

34 Chapel Lane. *Ballantrae*

In 1970 David Irvine built a small cottage on concrete block pilings for Dr. and Mrs. Fritz (Lynn) Englehart of Trenton, New Jersey. The Engleharts had rented #42 for many years while their children, Skip, Nancy and Carol, were growing up.

BALLANTRAE

It was Fritz Engelhart who organized the then-existing five cottage owners to invest $1000 each to go along with his $5000 to assist the Irvines in buying Harbour View from Walter Flett.

In 1981 Virginia Barrie Squiers of Sarasota, Florida bought the cottage from the Englehart estate and immediately added the south wing to it. She named the resulting cottage *Ballantrae* in remembrance of the Barrie family home in Scarsdale.

In 1986-87 she built a full basement under the existing structure and totally remodeled the interior, making it an all-weather, year-round house with built-in two-car garage and full guest apartment. They put in their own well and, with 4-wheel drive vehicles, can occupy the house comfortably in mid-winter.

Mrs. Squiers was Virginia Barrie and had summered at Harbor View in the twenties and thirties, beginning at age three. Jim Squiers, who had first come to Harbour View at the age of 18 months, is Louise Odell's grandson. Their many earlier summers spent here notwithstanding, they had never been at Harbor View at the same time until they met here in 1947.

They married in 1954. They have a daughter, Priscilla Squiers, and son-in-law, Kyle Minor, who became the proud parents of a son, Kieran, in 1996.

#45—5 Cottage Lane

Built 1903. Steelman cabin in 1931.

The original cabin was torn down except for the chimney, and a small cottage was built in its place. It was bought by Hugh Smith in 1981 for his mother, Mrs. Whipple ("Pat") Ridgway and expanded to include a spacious kitchen.

After Dr. Ridgway's death, Mrs. Ridgway married Dr. Herman Rhu of Tucson, Arizona in 1990.

In 1996 ownership of the cottage was transferred to Mrs. Rhu's daughter, Barbara Wilkins.

#47—184 Harbour View Road

Flint cabin in 1931. Built ca. 1903. The Flints were from Rochester, NY, Mr. Flint being connected with Kodak. Their children were Betty, Myra and Kimball. They were keen tennis players and at least eight or ten years older than I was.

This cabin was nearly identical to #41, and has also been remodeled. Its style, except for the siding (both originally had vertical log siding), has been kept like the original.

It was bought from the Irvines by Tiffin Shenstone (Allen Shenstone's second wife), who planned to remodel it and live in it. However, when the Mathers cottage became available in 1969, she bought it and gave #47 to her daughters, Daisy and Katherine.

It is now owned by Katherine's sons, Christopher and Lawrence Mead of Albuquerque, New Mexico.

#48—190 Harbour View Road

In 1931 Dr. and Mrs. Allen Shenstone of Princeton, New Jersey owned the cottage. The Shenstone cottage was one of the first cottages to be built to order for Harbor View people and to be privately owned. It was built by Allen Shenstone's father in 1906 on the site of the original Daniel Sulis, Jr. farmhouse.

This was the first Ralph Cossitt cottage at Harbor View. It has been continuously owned by the Shenstone family.

Allen Shenstone, then of Toronto, met his first wife, Molly, in England while in the army during World War I. Mrs. Shenstone, a splendid watercolorist, died in 1966 and Allen remarried in 1968. Tiffin (Harper), the new Mrs. Shenstone, didn't like the cottage.

Present owner Mr. and Mrs. Michael (Susan) Shenstone of Ottawa. Fifth generation children now enjoy visiting. Michael and Susan Shenstone's children: Thomas, Barbara and Mary.

#49. Twin Cabin in 1931

So named because its right and left ends were mirror images. Twin Cabin was torn down because the bank beneath had eroded and the building, hanging over the edge of the bluff, was unsafe. The twin cabin site is now vacant.

25 Cottage Lane

In 1950 Ralph Cossitt built a cottage just up from #49 for Dr. and Mrs. Evatt (Rita) Mathers of Halifax, designed by Mrs. Mathers.

Dr. Mathers had been a young MD (ophthalmologist) at the time of the Halifax Explosion in 1918 and cared for many of the eye injuries that resulted from it.

The cottage was so attractive that soon afterwards Ralph Cossitt was hired to build a duplicate of it up on the Old Post Road.

Dr. Allen Shenstone and his second wife, Tiffin, occupied the Mathers cottage until it was inherited by Tiffin's daughter, Daisy Fitch.

Val and Daisy Fitch of Princeton, New Jersey now have the cottage. Curiously, both Dr. Allen Shenstone and Dr. Val Fitch were head of the Physics Department at Princeton University, but at different times.

The cabin is now owned by Mrs. Fitch's three children: Douglas Harper Wilkinson of Chesterfield, New Hampshire; Elisha Sharp of Capulin, New Mexico; and Locke (Mrs. John) Harvey of Baltimore, Maryland. Mrs. Fitch has seven granddaughters.

#50—194 Harbour View Road. *Perryford*

From a sketch drawn by Mr. Harry W. Ford, Daly John built this cottage for the Ford family in 1909. This was on land purchased from Bishop Jaggar and also technically was not originally part of Harbor View.

Ralph Cossitt was one of the four men who built the cottage. Construction took two months. Cossitt finished the job by himself and did all the trim.

The interior trim throughout is yellow birch with the bark left on. Mr. Cossitt selected the birch in the woods and cut it in the winter when the sap was down so that the bark would stick tight. This was the first use of yellow birch as trim, and the interior of the chapel was patterned after it.

He also designed and built all the furniture, using Douglas fir boards and yellow birch, ash and poplar, all with the bark left on. He selected each piece of wood for its natural curvature and taper.

Ten years later Ralph Cossitt added a verandah to the cottage, and, later still, the back bedroom.

The Ford property, then called *Tuckaway*, was one of the great show-places of Nova Scotia because the Fords spent nearly all their time and that of Mr. Potter, their full-time gardener, on their flower gardens.

One time there was tension close to bloodshed over the Fords' prize dahlias. That occurred when someone left Miss Jaggar's gate open and her cows ate most of the dahlias. Mr. Potter and Miss Jaggar's herdsman came close to blows over the incident.

So intense a gardener was Harry W. Ford that no visitors were welcome on his property unless they were there to see or work in the gardens.

After Mr. Ford's death, the cottage was inherited by son H. Webster Ford. Webster was an Olympic runner who had the great misfortune to lose a leg due to tuberculosis of the bone and thus was deprived of the activity that he most valued.

His wife, the former Marjorie Olcott of Maplewood, New Jersey, was highly esteemed by her neighbors at Harbour View.

Webster died in 1963 and Marjorie sold the place the following year to Elmer and Rellen Perry of Charlottesville, Virginia. They renamed it *Perryford*.

Mr. Perry, an engineer, finished the attic himself with Douglas fir paneling and bookcases. Ralph Cossitt named it the "Bear's Den."

As was the case with the Richardson/Prescesky cottage, erosion of the bluff on which the cottage sits is worrisome to the Perrys. To retard the inevitable, they have succeeded in keeping the bluff heavily covered with trees and alders, only cutting notches here and there through which to enjoy the magnificent view.

Perryford is now owned by Dr. Christopher Perry and is occupied mainly by his mother, Rellen (Mrs. Elmer V.) Perry. Christopher and his wife, Antoinette, live in Montreal.

#51 (at the end of Harbour View Road) This was the Richardson cottage in 1931.

The Richardsons, Archbishop John A. and Mrs. Dora, built at the top of the sandy bluff facing Digby Gut on land purchased from Bishop Jaggar, thus technically the property was never part of the original Harbor View colony.

The cottage was built by Ralph Cossitt in 1911.

Bishop Richardson died in 1938. After the Richardsons' time the property was bought by Mr. Ford, and the bishop's study was moved behind the Ford cottage. Then the Fords sold the Richardson place in 1956 to the Prescesky family of Montreal (Peter and Erika, with their children Michael, Stephen, John, Andrew, Douglas, Jill, Nancy, Pam and Elizabeth.)

Eventually ownership went to Andrew. He had the cottage moved back 150 feet from the brink of the fast-eroding bluff to its present position, and placed on a proper concrete foundation, had a new stone chimney and fireplace built, and partially remodeled the interior. Over the years the bluff had suffered severe erosion and just before the cottage was moved back it was only a few feet from the edge.

In October 1995 Beowulf Klebert of Vienna, Austria, bought the house at auction. He had it gutted and completely remodeled and winterized. He has two sons, Sebastian and Philip, who presently reside in Tokyo.

234 Jaggar Lane

Russell Fries, son of Hester and Mills Fries and presently of Alexandria, Virginia, bought the land from Walter Flett in 1967. He and his first wife, Sylvia, built the house on it in 1972. They have a son, Thomas, and a daughter, Gwyneth.

In 1993 Russell married Ann Erdman of Princeton, New Jersey, who brought to the marriage her children, Lynne Erdman and Lealea (Mrs. Thomas) Marshall.

Anticipation

Bob Milbank writes:

> Every summer, after arriving at Yarmouth and starting off for Smith's Cove, I would see the bright sun, the blue sky, the water, the land, and the beautiful Nova Scotia flowers with their pastel and vivid colors. And I would think about how much fun I had at Harbor View last year, and a certain feeling would come over me, as it does now. And I would recall a favorite poem by William Wordsworth that begins:
>
>> My heart leaps up when I behold
>> A rainbow in the sky:
>> So it was when my life began;
>> So is it now I am a man,
>> So be it when I shall grow old.

This in not the end of The Harbour View Story. Someone may step forward and write another chapter or two about the year 2020, or completely revise the foregoing text. I guarantee it will be an enjoyable project.[5]

---

5   *The Harbour View Story Continues*, with stories from all the cottage families, was completed in 2024.

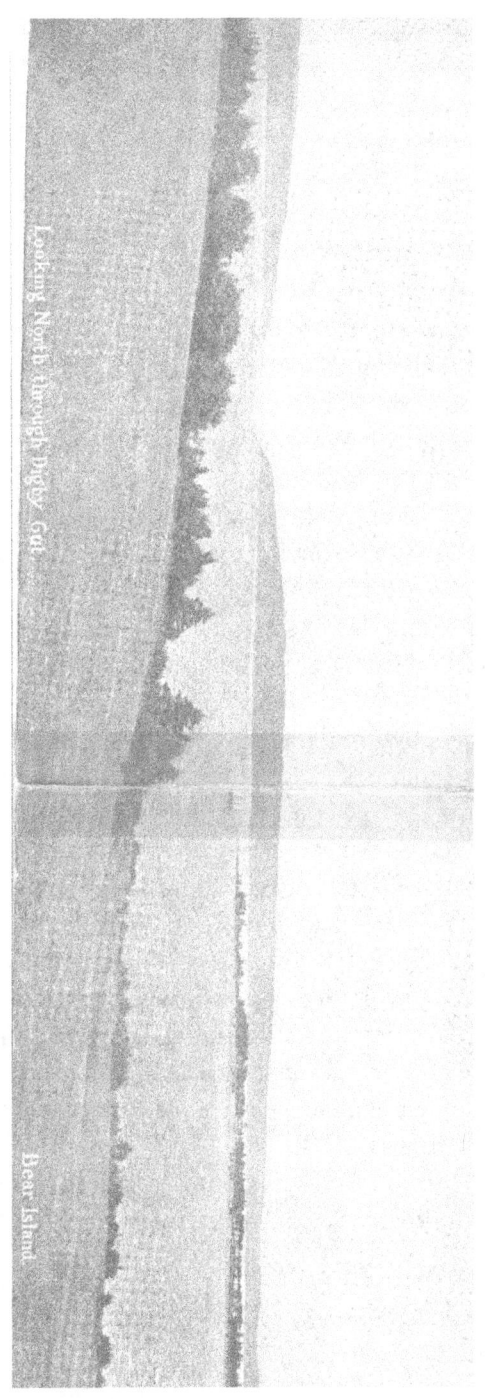

Looking North through Digby Gut.

Bear Island

The view from Argonaut Hill toward Digby Gut

About the author

Charles Turnbull was a lifelong summer resident of Harbour View, his lanky frame and friendly demeanor a fixture in the life of the community for decades. He treasured and maintained *Sunnymeade*, the cottage that his grandmother built in 1928, and always took keen interest in the people and activities of the community, from the days  of his boyhood and beyond. It is thanks to the combination of his habits of acute observation, his remarkable memory and his desire to keep the history of this special place alive that this book exists.

Charles was born in 1923, the oldest son of an American mother and a Canadian father descended from a forebear who settled in Digby in 1786. He was raised in New Jersey and went to McDonogh School and Wesleyan University. He spent his adult years in New Jersey and Connecticut with his wife, Priscilla, where they raised three children.

His career was in engineering, but, in keeping with his interest in many other pursuits, he was highly productive as an artist and an author, having published seven books and two essays.

He died in 2016.

This volume is a tribute to an entire community, a place more special to him than anywhere else on earth.

www.ingramcontent.com/pod-product-compliance
Lightning Source LLC
Chambersburg PA
CBHW071158120626
46546CB00006B/2321